W0259808

Against Identity

Against Identity

The Wisdom of Escaping the Self

ALEXANDER DOUGLAS

ALLEN LANE
an imprint of
PENGUIN BOOKS

ALLEN LANE

UK | USA | Canada | Ireland | Australia
India | New Zealand | South Africa

Allen Lane is part of the Penguin Random House group of companies whose addresses can be found at global.penguinrandomhouse.com.

Penguin Random House UK
One Embassy Gardens, 8 Viaduct Gardens, London SW11 7BW

penguin.co.uk

First published in Great Britain by Allen Lane 2025
003

Set in 12/14.75pt Dante MT Std
Typeset by Jouve (UK), Milton Keynes
Printed and bound in Great Britain by Clays Ltd, Elcograf S.p.A.

The authorized representative in the EEA is Penguin Random House Ireland, Morrison Chambers, 32 Nassau Street, Dublin D02 YH68

A CIP catalogue record for this book is available from the British Library

ISBN: 978–0–241–64821–6

Penguin Random House is committed to a sustainable future for our business, our readers and our planet. This book is made from Forest Stewardship Council® certified paper.

To my wife, Lauren Douglas:
We are Zhuang Zhou, and we are the butterfly.

Contents

Introduction: Identity Kills

Long ago, in a mythical realm in what is now China,[1] there were three emperors: Shu, Hu and Hundun. Shu was the Emperor of the Southern Sea. Hu was the Emperor of the Northern Sea. Between them was the Centre – the territory of Hundun. The two emperors of the seas frequently met in the Centre, where Hundun always welcomed them with perfect hospitality. Shu and Hu, like us, had openings in their heads: eyes, ears, mouth and nostrils. Hundun, however, had none. He was blank and featureless. One day, Shu and Hu decided to bore holes into him, so that he too could have features like theirs. Each day, they drilled a new hole. And on the seventh day, Hundun died.

One clue to the meaning of this mysterious story lies in the name *Hundun* (*hun* 混 *dun* 沌, or 'mixture', 'chaos'). The meaning evoked is something like 'roly-poly' or 'hotchpotch'. Pronounced in Cantonese, it is 'wonton' – the name of the famous Chinese dumplings, which can wrap up a variety of fillings.[2] Thus, Hundun's name implies that even though he is unformed, he contains potential forms, as an uncarved block contains all the shapes a sculptor could make from it.[3] Some scholars therefore suppose that this story might be a parody of older creation myths, which often represent the formation of the cosmos from chaos, illustrated through the murder or casting out of a wayward figure personifying chaos.[4] In this case, Hundun personifies the primal chaos from which the cosmos is formed, through the violently creative act of Shu and Hu.

But I find in Hundun's story something more personal. It is the story of each one of us. Hundun's facelessness is a metaphor for a lack of definite identity.[5] In puncturing Hundun, Shu and Hu give him an identity by which he can be recognized. But in the process, Hundun dies. This is the story of how we receive identity from our peers and how, when we do so, something is destroyed within us. The power of the undefined is lost by being forced into something definite. Our inner being is not a blank emptiness; it is an all-embracing multiplicity: Hundun is wonton. *Against Identity* is about how our inner Hundun can be revived, and how destructive the process of losing it can be.

This book examines a *philosophy* in the ordinary sense of the word: a certain way of looking at life and the world. Good philosophy should provide us with a feeling of clarity and ease – a new understanding and an ability to navigate life wisely.

The philosophy studied here is found in the works of three thinkers, writing in entirely different cultures and times. We start by contemplating the ancient East Asian philosopher Zhuangzi (pronounced in modern Mandarin as 'joo-ang zuh'),[6] before moving on to the Dutch Republic (perhaps the first modern nation) with philosopher Benedict de Spinoza, and then, finally, we arrive in the near contemporary period, with twentieth-century French theorist René Girard. I propose that all three thinkers faced similar problems in their lifetimes and diagnosed the same ills in their society, which led them to develop strikingly similar philosophies against identity.

The philosophy I find in all three thinkers can be sketched out as follows. Each of us is born with a deep biological urge for self-preservation. But consciously pursuing self-preservation requires some notion of who or what our *self* is. Here is our predicament. In the beginning, we are not sure of who we are.

Some believe that we can find out by introspecting and looking within to find our true self. But Zhuangzi, Spinoza and Girard disagree. Look within, they would say, and you will find a mess. Introspection reveals only a confusion of qualities. There is no map highlighting which qualities truly define us: which are our defining traits and which our fleeting states. Nor does *who you happen to be right now* define who you *essentially* are. You might not yet have become your true self – and you may still have the enigma of yourself to solve, as Saint Augustine put it.[7]

Since introspection reveals nothing, we have no choice but to look *outwards*, to *others* – real or fictional – as models of our true being. Find the ones who stir your admiration and take them as exemplars for your best self. We do this as children, when we play at being superheroes, parents, monsters, criminals, police. We do not stop when we grow up. It just stops being a game. When people say, 'I know who I am', what they mean is that they know who *somebody else* is. They have decided to be that: a borrowed self to fill the blank inside. But this – our profound ontological unoriginality – is an embarrassing fact, which we go to some lengths to hide from ourselves. Proving the theory that drives this philosophy therefore requires more than just rational argument. It is also necessary to overcome some of our psychological defence mechanisms. 'Individualism is a formidable lie,' as Girard said.[8]

The reappearance of this same philosophy in diverse times and places suggests that it is a piece of wisdom transcending local culture. But the three epochs that Zhuangzi, Spinoza and Girard lived through have something important in common. They were all eras in which a social order had fallen apart, or was falling apart. Zhuangzi wrote his major works sometime during the Warring States period of pre-China, following the collapse of a great empire and its associated social hierarchy.

Spinoza conceived his main ideas in the Dutch Republic, following the breakup of Western Christendom and at the beginning of capitalist modernity. And Girard worked in France and the United States in the later twentieth century, where new ideals of self-invention arose in the ruins of the Second World War, the process of decolonization, and a revolution in media technology.

In each of these ages, philosophies of individualism developed, celebrating and justifying the power of individuals to decide *who to be*, newly liberated from regimes of social control. The philosophy examined here warns of the danger of these individualistic philosophies and presents an alternative. The alternative is not a reversion to a traditional social order. Rather, it aims to understand how identity is formed, in order to escape it altogether.

Some psychologists distinguish between *identity* and *self.* Your identity is a specific concept of your persona, role or social position. Your self is the subject that inhabits and operates your identity.[9] But selves are always known under identities. To know any object, we must identify it under some concept or description. 'Self' and 'identity' are thus often used interchangeably in this book, though occasionally it is recognized that there is a portion of the self that eludes – and exists beyond – any identity. The starting point of the philosophy explored here is the theory that *identity* – the concept or description under which the self is known – comes from the observation of others. The process by which essential identity is thus modelled and then imposed is destructive. Really it is a form of spiritual violence, which often leads to violence of a more concrete kind.[10] It is also an ultimately doomed enterprise. No matter how deeply you push yourself into your chosen essential identity, there will always be some residue that refuses to be absorbed – some remainder that cannot be resolved.[11] This is the portion of the self that lies, always, beyond identity.

The way out of this destructive and unsatisfying predicament must be by tracing the problem to its root: our original hunger for *being*. Since mere being is an empty concept, *wanting to be* must mean wanting to *find your true identity*, which can only come from outside of us. If we were instead to strive to overcome the hunger for identity, then we could remain happily indefinite and enjoy whatever concatenation of accidents happens to be bestowed upon us by external circumstances and spontaneous inner drives.

This is how we can understand the story of Hundun's death. The faceless, indefinite, identityless Hundun is amicable and hospitable. Shu and Hu meet in his territory because, perhaps, they are rivals to each other, and Hundun's territory is neutral ground. Hundun avoids getting caught up in their conflict and is welcoming to both sides, perhaps because of his lack of identity. By piercing Hundun, Shu and Hu commit him to a distinct identity, a desire driven by the fact that they have faces themselves. They want to work out who he is, perhaps to decide whose side he is really on. Hundun represents everything in us that is unique and undefinable, impossible to fully capture in any concept or definition, impossible to recruit to any collective identity.[12] Imposing identity upon us reduces us to what can be defined and recognized. Stamping somebody with a face kills the Hundun in them.

Identity, however, is not merely destructive. It also provides moral guidance in our lives. Knowing *who you are* provides a sense of *what you should do* in a given situation.[13] Zhuangzi, Spinoza and Girard go further and propose that it is *only* through identity that we decide what to do. They hold to a theory of *metaphysical desire*. The theory is, roughly, that while our basic appetites are biologically determined, our desires beyond these basic appetites arise from a fundamental psychological drive for identity – a drive to *be a certain sort of person*. What we desire is, first of all, to *be* something rather than to *possess* something or *do* something.[14] I want to eat because I want to be a thriving organism; I want to eat *foie gras* because I want to be a member of a certain social group; I want to listen to black metal music because I strive to *be the sort of person* who listens to this genre – to have that identity, often with the clothes to match.

Why I should strive for one particular identity rather than another is not yet clear. But we can understand why I should want *some* identity. If I am not someone or other, I can feel like I am nobody – or nothing in particular. I can suffer from what psychologists call an 'identity deficit'.[15] As Spinoza puts it in his philosophical masterpiece, *Ethics Demonstrated in Geometrical Order* (1677), each thing strives 'to persevere in its being' (*Ethics*, 3p6). But here 'its being' refers to essential identity. After all, surviving cannot just mean remaining in existence as *anything whatsoever*, otherwise turning into a corpse would count as surviving. Surviving means remaining as what you *truly* or *essentially* are. Some notion of essential identity is necessary to define what you are striving to be, and to remain as. Desires grow from the root of this striving. You decide who you are, and then this determines how you want to act, what you want to possess, who you want to connect with, what you want to believe.

Identity also serves an important social function. Anthropologists studying human violence have proposed that there are two quite different types of violence.[16] We humans seem to have developed our special ability to avoid one sort of violence by harnessing the power of another. The first sort is known as *reactive* violence, an antisocial kind of violence that flouts the rules and conventions that govern a society – violence that is illegal, impolite, or in some way 'not the done thing'. The second sort, *proactive* violence, is violence used to police and enforce the same rules and conventions. Human communities use proactive violence to punish and discourage reactive violence, forming coalitions to punish those who break the rules. But since we cannot always observe each other's *behaviour*, societies in practice police the *identities* of their members. Those whose character makes them seem likely to transgress, who do not seem to be *the right sort of person*, are far more likely to be accused of breaking the rules and often punished as a precautionary measure.

Identity management is thus part of how communities are governed and maintained. Passing through the social filter without being targeted for proactive violence requires us to maintain a healthy profile as a friend of the community. Developing an identity – the right sort of identity – is necessary to avoid proactive violence, although in modern communities genuine violence can be replaced by more insidious psychological warfare. Yet the process by which identity is imposed is also a sort of violence, illustrated in the story of Hundun. All three thinkers studied here believed that violence is found at the origin of most social institutions. The Hundun story has been read as a warning for how humans are initiated into social institutions and what is lost in the process: it is a fable of a fall and loss of innocence.[17]

Identity is not just produced by violence; it also inspires it. This is because it is tied up with distinction and comparison. To identify yourself is also, inevitably, to identify *others*. Shu and Hu could not have faces without feeling the need to give one to Hundun. If you define yourself by your ethnicity or your taste in music, then you *ipso facto* demarcate yourself against others who do not share in that identity. Here we have the basis for division and intergroup conflict. Groups that identify themselves – whether by ethnicity, politics, clothing, sports teams, opinions on metaphysics, or precise predictions of the consequences of economic policy – easily end up at war with groups that identify differently.

One reason for this is simple enough. Intelligent people often turn out to be surprisingly unresponsive to valid arguments and solid evidence. But for many people, their beliefs and practices *define who they are*. They belong to their essential identity. And since, as we have seen, surviving means remaining as what you essentially are, threats to such essential beliefs and practices appear as threats to survival. Arguments and evidence are up against something much more powerful than they can ever be: the fear of death, the survival instinct. Threatening your identity is threatening your very being.

Thus, the thirst for identity brings the constant risk of violence. When pursuing goal x is part of the essential identity of one group, and pursuing goal y – inconsistent with x – is part of the essential identity of another, then the groups are in a war of extermination. The goals x and y might not seem particularly important, yet by becoming entrenched in the identities of the combatants they take on existential significance. Winning becomes a matter of survival.

In such cases physical violence might not occur, but the tone of the disagreement will match that of a violent conflict. Belligerents can experience disagreement *as* violence: threats to ideas that define their very being. They will feel no hesitation in throwing out taunts, insults and condemnations. These harsh tactics make much more sense than rational argument, once we recognize what the stakes are. If changing somebody's mind requires you to change *who they think they are*, then what you need is not rational arguments but ways to undermine your opponents' sense of self or self-respect. Aggression, performative contempt, public humiliation – anything that might fill the targets with enough shame to want to be somebody else – these are the right tools for the job.

Put bluntly, the struggle for identity is what leads people to fight so brutally over minutiae or matters that seem much too uncertain to be definite about. We find here a powerful diagnosis of our philosophical sickness.

Our philosophical sickness is manifested in many ways. At present, a hot political topic is *polarization*. The theme of the 2023–4 United Nations Human Development Report is 'reimagining cooperation in a polarized world'.[18] The report explains how people become polarized when they incorporate political opinions into their identities.[19] If your whole identity is based on a political opinion, then you are likely to develop an extreme version of it, just as somebody who makes exercise their whole identity will progress inexorably from 10k park runs to ultra-triathlons, while someone who makes recreational cannabis their whole identity will end up with t-shirts, wallets, bumper stickers and bongs emblazoned with the sacred leaf. When your political beliefs become part of who you are, anyone who disagrees, or even anyone insufficiently interested in the topic, is at risk of a heated conversation or an uninvited lecture.

In the case of political views, the UN report explains how polarization is a serious barrier to collective action. People can hardly work or compromise with others when their entire identity is based on opposing them. Identity stops the world from working together to solve its common problems. It also makes people vulnerable to misinformation, thus reinforcing polarization by making each party feel like all the facts are on their side. Healthy scepticism about confirming evidence is hardly compatible with an identity-driven need to hold a certain belief or attitude.

To draw an example from my own experience, during a dispute over UK higher education pensions, driven by legitimate concerns over some proposed reforms, I saw one professor tweet a wild misinterpretation of her pension statement. She somehow inferred that her *total* retirement income would be £3700 per year. This attracted a chorus of outraged and supportive commentary. But the figure quoted was much less than the professor was paying in contributions per year, let alone what her employer was contributing. If both employee and employer were really paying in much more than the pension was due to pay out, why would the professor not have put the same money into savings instead? Why did the crowd of supportive and outraged academics – specialists in rigorous thinking – not ask this question, or at least recommend to the professor that she withdraw from a scheme that, apparently, lost all of her employer's contributions and some of her own? Why did they not wonder whether, perhaps, there might have been a mistake in her calculation?

The reason, I think, is that the dispute had become so polarized that outrage about pensions had become an identity for many academics: it defined their sense of self-worth in the face of an attack by consecutive governments intent on reducing their public funding. They were ready to believe anything to retain that identity, even things that patently made no sense. I have no doubt that I have believed equally absurd things in the pursuit of a particular political identity. Or rather, I have *expressed* such beliefs; when it comes to identity, we often do not get as far as thinking about whether we can really imagine the beliefs we loudly profess to as actually being true.[20] Political commitments, often reasonable in themselves, can lead us to agree with nearly anything said by those we take to be on our side. Here, I chose to spotlight an elite group – academics – to show that neither education nor intelligence makes the mind more resistant to polarization. Even when people have the most to gain from working together, they instead polarize into warring tribes and twist the facts to show that they are right and good, while their opponents are wrong, stupid and evil.

Both philosophy and life tell me that this fight for and against identity is universal across humanity. I was raised in a multiethnic household and grew up on different continents – Australia, Asia and North America, eventually ending up in Europe – and in that time, I have been more struck by the deep similarities among people than their superficial differences. My parents set the example of delighting in, rather than resenting, those differences. But I have also experienced all these cultures as an outsider. I first left my native country, Australia, as a young child, and I am not even very *native* to Australia – my mother was a first-generation immigrant from Macau, and my father's family had only migrated from Scotland a few generations back. Being an outsider makes it difficult to succeed in the specific status-game of culture. First you have to learn what the game is. Moving from understated, self-effacing, indirect Java, it took me a while to understand the bold, explicit game of self-promotion required in Washington DC. Initially I could not control whether I signalled the healthy ambition and self-belief that was expected of me or arrogant showboating that nobody liked; to me they looked the same. Returning to Australia for university required a talk from my father about what we call

'Tall Poppy Syndrome' – the cool reception that would greet the American-style earnestness I had only recently learned.

An outsider is also subject to competing pressures. In addition to constantly learning what new peer groups expected, I had to weigh up the expectations of my family, itself dividing into different cultures with different expectations, reading my behaviour in different ways.

Cultural outsiders tend to cope by going in one of two directions. Either they throw themselves into beating the indigenous at their own game, rapidly mastering new techniques of status and identity, or they try to take advantage of their outside perspective to escape the game altogether. After a series of embarrassing failures with the first strategy, I was left with the second. I believe the philosophers that I present here went the same way. The *Zhuangzi*, written around 476–221 BCE in what is now China, is full of favourable presentations of dropouts, criminals, beggars and outcasts, suggesting that its author(s) were outsiders by choice. Spinoza was doubly displaced: the child of Jewish migrants who fled to the Dutch Republic, who was then expelled from his own community as a young adult.[21] Girard was a quintessential outsider: a French expatriate in the United States and a practising Catholic among a milieu of secular postmodernist intellectuals. He once said: 'All my life, I've never been able to work except outside institutions and so, subconsciously, I worked against them.'[22]

Perhaps this is only a self-serving narrative, but I believe that outsiders have a unique perspective on the question of identity. Those born native to a culture seem to me to fall easily into the illusion that their drive to cultivate a certain identity arises from deep within themselves – that their ambitions and aspirations are the feeling of their true self bubbling up from the individual soul and demanding expression in the world. From the outside, it is apparent how much these ambitions and aspirations are in fact imposed upon individuals by the prevailing culture, as Hundun's face was drilled into him by the other emperors. The outsider can see how intensely people imitate each other and compete to express the same identities. The outsider can also see how identity-formation is driven by fear and implicit threats: we 'find ourselves' under duress from a crowd that demands to know who we are and will deal with us according to the answer. And the outsider can stand back and ask whether this whole process makes anyone happy.

It is hard to see how the pursuit of identity can lead to happiness. The inner self that we long to express is, in the first instance, modelled on an ideal found in our cultural environment. Whatever this identity might be – SUV-flaunting corporate lawyer, indigenous-art-buying diversity consultant, career politician at the top of the pyramid, or responsible citizen relentlessly educating those of feebler virtue – each is guaranteed to serve as *an exemplar*, and will possess the quality of *exemplarity*. Striving to be like our model, we will desire to become exemplary ourselves. This means seeking out admirers or disciples of our own, just as our model found a disciple in us. Unfortunately, others are not looking to become our emulators. On the contrary, they will want to retain their own hard-won identities and, propelled by the same dynamic, to attract emulators of their own. We end up in a sort of existential power struggle in which each wishes to be emulated and none wants to emulate. Everyone wants to be the influencer, nobody the influenced: and so the public sphere becomes a theatre with all actors and no audience, a fashion show with everyone on the catwalk, a university with lecturers and no students, an ashram with gurus and no disciples.

Moreover, we work in a limited-attention economy. Public

admiration is a scarce resource because the attention span of the public is limited, as most people broadcast more than they receive. Different aspiring exemplars must compete for the approval of a highly inattentive crowd. Social interactions become a complex, competitive game of pride, envy and ambition, where the stake is survival – survival, again, meaning *retention of identity*. Influencing others becomes integral to its goal.

Not only does this lead to rivalry and conflict; it leads to frustration. What we wanted was our *own* identity. What we keep finding is *somebody else's*, and maintaining it feels less like self-expression than pandering to the crowd. No wonder we kick so hard against those who threaten our identity. They take the blame for a failure whose real explanation lies in the fundamental inconsistency of our aim. They remind us of the embarrassing arbitrariness of what we take to be essential – of our ontological unoriginality, our essential emptiness. When they thump against us, we are ashamed to ring hollow.

All we can do to drown out this unwelcome reminder is drive ourselves harder into our aspiring identity: to be bigger and bolder in expressing it. That is exhausting and expensive. It costs us in time, effort, stress and material resources (status symbols are costly to produce). No wonder we live in such a busy, competitive, anxious world, straining against the limits of what an alien visitor might regard as enviously abundant natural resources and great ingenuity in enhancing them. No wonder millions of lives are destroyed in wars over empty abstractions like national honour. No wonder sensible institutions are torn down for the sake of a politician's career aspirations or for one political tribe to prove a point to its recalcitrant rivals. No wonder everyone rails against the unchecked power of giant corporations while giving those same corporations unlimited access to their fragile self-esteem and nervous ambition, ready for conversion into endless purchases.

Most of all, we find ourselves unable to adapt – to each other, to the rhythms of nature, to the inevitability of change. Identities are formed in the past, but life drives us into the future. When our current ways of life prove unsustainable, you might think that we could just change them – after all, there are many worthwhile ways to live, and being forced to change is often a blessing in disguise. But if our current way of life has become part of *who we think we are*, then changing it means losing our being; it might as well be death.

If a superpower nation finds its global dominance challenged, you might think that it would welcome the break, letting others take the reins for a while. But if superpower status has become part of its national identity, then it will prefer war without end to a comfortable seat on the back bench of nations.[23]

When the economic tide turns against somebody on the Forbes list of the world's richest people, you might think that they could drop out and retire to a life of luxurious leisure. Instead, they work harder, take greater risks, or increase the criminality of their activities to restore yield.

When we and our political rivals suddenly find ourselves in common difficulty, you might think that we could put aside our differences and find solidarity in a shared struggle. But then we would lose our tribal identity: better to both lose as opposing sides than both win and risk merging into the people we have defined ourselves by hating.

When an intelligent species finds that its current energy base is thoroughly unsuitable to its long-term needs, you might think it would quickly move to transform it. But human individuals and communities have internalized current patterns of production and consumption into their own identities, making even small reforms appear as threats to their very being and large reforms politically impossible. Moreover, no group wants to make a sacrifice if there is even a chance that some rival group is getting a better deal: better a level playing field at the bottom of the ocean than any slight to our honour and status. Since perfect justice is impossible, let the heavens fall.

Thus, do we lock ourselves into unsustainable patterns, in hopeless denial of the fundamental instability of things, not because change is painful or difficult (after all, so is failing to change), but because our identity has made it logically impossible. We have become what we do, and so what we do cannot change, even when it must.

One symptom of the identity drive, therefore, is hyperactivity. We consume vast quantities of materials and energy trying to control events and each other – trying to make the world match the pattern consistent with our sense of self. Few philosophies enjoy less popularity in practice than what Daoist texts call *wu wei* 無為 – or non-action.[24] Of course, there are many things to be done in the world. The poor must be lifted out of poverty, the sick must be treated, broken systems must be fixed, outdated ways of doing things must be reformed when circumstances change. But there is a great deal of activity that occurs only for the sake of *extremification*: gaining more wealth for the rich, more power for the powerful, more beauty for the beautiful, more popularity for the popular, more hegemony for the hegemonic, more status for the elite, more education for the already overeducated (here I am not innocent), more medals to pin onto chests already crowded. All this activity is driven by identity. People begin to achieve outstanding, glorious identities and then see others catching up. To retain their glorious status, an integral part of their being, they run to stay ahead, with the competitors hot on their heels.

Imagine if we could stop, even for a moment, trying to be *anything*. Could we then find new ways to act and live, consistent with a changing world? Could we raise our gaze from the inner easel on which we were so furiously painting our self-portrait and see the beautiful world around us, celebrating its capacity to defy all our categories, expectations and attempts at control? Could we learn to see each other, not as the backdrop to our own self-portrait but as subjects of a wonderful and multifarious tableau, of which we make up just one small but vital part? Could we then do the one thing that every creature that has ever endured in our world has done – every species that made it through an extinction-level event, every culture that survived a colonial invasion, every individual who came out the other side of grief or a life-changing trauma – could we learn to adapt?

The hardest thing I have experienced in my life so far is watching my father in the early stages of Alzheimer's disease. His humour, wisdom and kindness were still there, but now they shone through clouds of confusion. My mother harnessed her linguistic gifts to sift grains of sense from his thought. The love was beautiful but heartbreaking.

To me, my father had always been defined by his bravery and intelligence. He always knew what to do, and he never let the situation get the better of him, no matter how hard things got. Wandering through the parks of London with him, listening to his strange rhapsody of blended past and future, of expertly identified trees alongside garbled fantasy-Latin, seeing the fear in his face as he realized what was happening to him, I worried that his core traits were, for the first time, under threat – from an invisible, interior enemy. I was losing him, I missed him, and I could not imagine going on without him. What my mother was going through I could not fathom.

Alzheimer's is a slow disease. Each time you adjust to one phase, it progresses to another. A friend told me I had to stop trying to bring my father back to my world and learn to enter his. That turned out to be the secret. My father was not vanishing; he was changing. He was continuing to teach me, even after losing the power of language. If he could learn to adapt to his strange new world, so could I. His personality dissolved, his appearance changed, but my love was the same. Nor did his love ever disappear; as I pushed him in his wheelchair and listened to his language breaking down from sentences to words to syllables, I felt it more than ever. He was becoming Hundun, and he was teaching me to become more like Hundun – letting go of the things I was exhausting myself trying to hold onto, the things by which I had defined both him and myself, and learning to find the joy in what was there.

This piece of wisdom shed new light on the philosophy I had been reading for years but not understanding. Nothing can stay the same. Trying to hold onto things the way they are is a losing game. But love remains, because love can flow along with the ways that things change. Love is as supple as the world, and the world's transformations cannot erase it. Love is the opposite of identity and the secret to adaptation.

Adaptation means changing, and changing means not needing to be the same. Not needing to be the same means not having a definite, immovable identity. It means giving up on trying to remake the world in your image – giving up, indeed, on having any image at all. It is thoroughly inconsistent with egotism and ambition. The philosophy presented here holds that the world needs less of those things and more of the love that penetrates to the deeper, uncarved layer of self and world. It holds up an ideal of reconnecting with the unpunctured, faceless Hundun.

Zhuangzi and Spinoza propose a way to achieve this, by deflecting our emulative tendencies towards a very different sort of exemplar. This exemplar is called '*Dao*' by Zhuangzi and 'God' by Spinoza. Both terms, I believe, refer to a fundamental undefined being, which these philosophers believe to underlie the well-defined reality perceived by our senses. This undefined being gives rise to all the definite things of the perceivable world by being determined into a vast variety of particular forms. Yet at another level it remains beyond all these particular things – beyond all determination. By emulating what I will call this *superdeterminate* being, we might reverse the pressures that drive us towards a definite identity. We might free ourselves from metaphysical desire and enter a life of peaceful contentment. We might feel a unity with others that is deeper than mere identification with them: seeing in them, not something *identical* to ourselves, but rather other expressions of the same superdeterminate being that we express. It shows the way that we can all be alike in difference – entering the world of others instead of trying to bring them into our own.

Against Identity is an exposition of this philosophy as found in these three thinkers – Zhuangzi, Spinoza and Girard. It will argue that this is an achievable goal, but it requires us to counter some of our deepest psychological tendencies, grounded in some of our most fundamental philosophical assumptions. It will also explore the question of how three such different worlds – the ancient Warring States, the modern Dutch Republic and postmodern France and California – produced such a strikingly similar philosophical position, one that runs so radically against our basic assumptions about human life and society. What allowed these thinkers to see danger in something as fundamental as the pursuit of identity? What allowed them to go much further than others who recognized the same danger – all the way to the goal of opposing identity wholesale?

The three thinkers would tell their own stories about the source of their ideas. For Zhuangzi, inspiration is said to be the cultivation and practice of *Dao*. For Spinoza, it is said to be the perfection of the intellect. For Girard, it is the Christian revelation. Is the deep similarity of their ideas a historical coincidence? Or was there, rather, something in the ages they lived through that radicalized them against identity? And what, then, might we learn from them?

One thing that is hard to miss is that all three of the ages through which these anti-identitarians lived were times in which, on the one hand, identity meant a great deal and, on the other, people faced genuine choices about their identity. Identity was not decided for them, as it had been in previous ages. People discovered a new-found freedom to choose their own path. But the freedom came with a cost. This reveals one way in which these thinkers, who saw things from the outside, might speak to us today. They present an alternative ethos to the identity-curation that is marketed to us so aggressively and for which we are so technologically well endowed. Rather than building profiles to fill the blank space of our fundamental indeterminacy, or hopelessly defying it as some existentialists suggest, we can make peace with this indeterminacy. Doing so might bring us tranquillity, within as well as without. Hundun was happy and generous before society attacked him with a face. And the world was at peace.

PART ONE

Zhuangzi

I.

'The Perfect Person Has No Identity'

Warring States

The *Zhuangzi* is a compilation of texts regarded, alongside the more famous *Dao De Jing*,[1] as canonical within the philosophical tradition known as Daoism or Taoism, which the *Stanford Encyclopedia of Philosophy* characterizes as follows:

> [Daoist] philosophical reflection engendered a distinctive ambivalence in advocacy – manifested in their indirect, non-argumentative style, their use of poetry and parable. In ancient China, the political implication of this Daoism was mainly an opposition to authority, government, coercion, and even to normal socialization in values. Daoist 'spontaneity' was contrasted with subtle or overt indoctrination in any specific or social *dao*.[2]

Dao 道 is a term notoriously difficult to translate. It refers to something like a way of being, thinking and acting. In the Daoist tradition it also refers to the *way of things* – the way that the cosmos seems to endlessly change and transform without any definite goal or endpoint, or concern for human ambitions.[3]

It is important to be aware, however, that 'Daoism' is a label that only started being applied long after the *Zhuangzi* was written. As the scholar A. C. Graham put it, 'Zhuangzi never knew he was a Daoist.'[4]

Tradition ascribes the *Zhuangzi* to the legendary figure Zhuang Zhou (roughly 'joo-ang jo-ooh' in modern Mandarin), said to have lived around the fourth century BCE. *Zhuangzi* (Master Zhuang) consists of writings expressive of Zhuang Zhou's thought, whether authored by him or not. Impossible to categorize, it is one of the strangest literary works from any culture, full of puzzling stories, philosophical conversations and paradoxical epigrams, matching Zhuangzi's received image as one of the most radically unconventional characters in human history. Most scholars now agree that these texts were not all composed by a single person or even in a single historical age.[5]

Zhuangzi, or Zhuang Zhou, is the legendary figure whose teachings and example inspire the texts that make up the book *Zhuangzi*. The book as we know it was compiled by the Neo-Daoist philosopher Guo Xiang (252–318 CE), and he also provided his own influential commentary on the book, which I will draw on in this part.[6] But despite these many contributing voices, I will choose to refer to the author of the text as simply 'Zhuangzi', following convention.

Very little is known about the real Zhuang Zhou. Historical records tell us that he came from the district of Meng in the state of Song (present-day Henan province), served in the lacquer garden (perhaps he was the keeper of a real lacquer-tree forest), and then abandoned this official position to lead a simple life in the wilderness.[7] There is a story that when some political official sent a messenger to offer him a position in government, Zhuangzi responded by asking whether the sacred tortoise, whose bones are preserved in the shrine of the king's ancestors, would not rather have been left alone to drag its tail in the mud (Z 17.31–2).[8] Perhaps this is how Zhuangzi wanted us to remember him: impervious to all ambition for honour and status, content as a simple tortoise in the dirt and clay. The text of the *Zhuangzi* is full of hermits, criminals, beggars and cripples, often favourably represented as characters who see through the many hypocrisies of their society. Both Zhuangzi and his philosophy conveyed the strong voice of a social outcast.

Zhuangzi is traditionally assigned the lifetime 369–286 BCE. If these dates are near to correct, he was born into the fallout of a great civilizational collapse: the demise of the Western Zhou empire. This empire had controlled what is now central China from around 1122 to 770 BCE. From its wreckage rival factions emerged, scrambling for power. Some aspired to found new nations and dynasties. They gave to this period its common name of 'Warring States' (*Zhanguo* 戰國). This was a period of uneasy transition. Social and political dissolution had eroded the old moral codes and political institutions, and upstarts were challenging the established positions of traditional rulers.[9] The number of cities is estimated to have multiplied by a factor of four between 600 and 250 BCE.[10] Frequent military conflict occurred among increasingly divided powers, while advances in metalworking led to improved weapons and more efficient agriculture, supporting larger, and well-armed, populations.[11]

In a sense, society was modernizing; and all modernization comes with feelings of anxiety about what the collapse of the old ways will bring. This unease can be felt in writings from this time. Several verses of lamentation from a very ancient anonymous collection of poetry, the *Classic of Poetry* or *shijing* 詩經 (11th–7th century BCE), convey a nervous sense of upheaval and unrest: 'Fragments and a remnant / Children of dispersion are we!'[12]

The Loss of Order

Philosophical writing from the time of the Warring States discusses questions of the social order and the possibility of morally educating human beings to fit defined roles and duties. Probably the most famous of these is the *Analects*, ascribed to Confucius – the Romanized name of *Kong Qiu* 孔丘 (ca. 551–479 BCE), who was the region's most influential philosopher. Confucius was such a famous figure that he features as a character in many of the stories of the *Zhuangzi*, sometimes as the object of parody, other times as the mouthpiece of profound wisdom. To understand the philosophical context of the *Zhuangzi*, we should look briefly at the philosophical problem Confucius aimed to solve.

The *Analects* is a collection of sayings by Confucius and stories about him. In one, Confucius is asked about *zheng* 政 – the governing sociopolitical order (we are not told precisely *what* he is asked about it) – and he replies: 'Let the ruler be a ruler, the subject a subject, the father a father, and the son a son.'[13] As a commentary by the much later scholar and Neo-Confucian Zhu Xi (1130–1200 CE) notes, Confucius did not believe this condition to be fulfilled in his time: the *zheng* 政 was gone, and rulers, subjects, fathers and sons had lost their way – the *dao* 道 mentioned above.[14] His anxiety is not simply over the prospect that, without *zheng* 政, sons would stop obeying fathers and subjects would stop obeying rulers. It is, rather, that fathers, sons, subjects and rulers would stop *being* fathers, sons, subjects and rulers altogether. Thus, his interlocutor replies: 'Splendid! Truly, if the ruler be not a ruler, the subject not a subject, the father not a father, the son not a son, then even if there be grain, would I get to eat it?' This implies that a successful sociopolitical order depends on well-defined social roles and rigid class distinctions, without which basic functions such as the distribution of food cannot be managed. The worry was that this order and the roles it was based on was collapsing.[15]

Defining social roles, however, requires us to know how people should be and act. The Warring States period opened to philosophers the question: 'What is the *dao* 道?' The Way, or the *dao* 道, is the appropriate mode of life, grounded in an understanding of what people are.[16] For Confucius, the *dao* 道 looked backwards, towards a better past – it symbolized the old social order and hierarchy that had developed during the age of the Zhou empire.[17] In the *Analects* (3:14), he declares: 'I am for the Zhou' (*wu cong Zhou* 吾從周), making clear his lament for the loss of the old order and his hopes to restore it.

But to others, the Warring States period might have appeared as a time of liberation as well as dissolution. People who had once been interpellated by identities based on gender, occupation, social position or family title, were no longer forced to act according to the traditional understanding of these roles. What, under the old regime, would have appeared as a logical contradiction or a strange riddle – a servant who is not a servant, a father who is not a father – had become a live possibility.

This new feeling of freedom is confirmed in another part of the *Analects*, where Confucius reports that his first act in government would be to *rectify names* – or *zheng ming* 正名.[18] What are we to make of this odd policy proposal? The character *zheng* 正 – or 'rectify' – is a radical in another character, *zheng* 政 (you can see the compressed 正 in the left half), which we have already seen stands for the sociopolitical order whose dissolution fuels Confucius's anxiety. Meanwhile 'names', *ming* 名, has a broad meaning that can encompass 'reputation', 'purpose' and 'role'. 'Rectifying names' can thus mean *making people play their proper roles.*[19] Confucius wanted to restore the roles prescribed by the older tradition – to be shaped by traditional values.[20] Yet he was so urgent in calling to restore them precisely because they were dissolving. As he saw it, *ming* 名 must be repaired and rectified.

Sincerity and Conformism

Confucius's campaign to rectify names shows his awareness of the socially controlling function of language and its symbols: the 'symbolic order' that would be of great interest to anthropologists and literary theorists in the twentieth century. A teacher of mine once told me that he had attended a conservative Catholic boys' boarding school whose motto was: *isti vir* – be a man! The framers of this motto almost certainly did not mean: 'be any sort of man, e.g. an effete communist'. Rather, the word '*vir*' – 'man' – was a symbol loaded with role ethics and social expectations. Likewise, the symbolic order Confucius aims to rectify is built out of role models for agents to emulate.[21]

Each name encodes a model or exemplar. 'Ruler' encodes the model ruler, 'father' the exemplary father, 'wife' the ideal wife, and so on.[22] A world in which names are rectified is one in which people hailed by these names properly emulate their models. Nor is it enough for them to emulate *insincerely*, going through the motions outwardly without inwardly identifying with their role. A father who is a father, in Confucius's sense, must really identify as a father. He must see the model father as defining what he fundamentally is, not just something he has to appear to be. Some scholars, borrowing a term from the twentieth-century American literary critic Lionel

Trilling,[23] have been led to call this a 'sincerity regime'.[24] The demand of this regime is not simply that we play our social roles; it is that we play them *sincerely* – that we fully identify with them.

We can say that Confucius's sincerity regime promotes a type of *conformism*. Conformism, in its ordinary usage, means people conforming to each other, not to historical models.[25] However, in many stories, Confucius appears as an eccentric character, peddling old-fashioned ideas running counter to the culture of his age – a nostalgic oddball, who stood out rather than conforming. Moreover, the strong individualism that is sometimes put forward as a distinguishing feature of modern Western society and contrasted with conformism involves its own type of conformity: that of *being true to yourself*, which means – what else could it mean? – conforming to a model of yourself. The model might be of your own devising (though later we will see problems with this conception), but conforming to it is still conforming. If a society that produces a figure as strange as Confucius is conformist, I would like to see a non-conformist society.

Zhuangzi: Against Identity

The same culture produced a figure much wilder than Confucius: Zhuangzi, who was, as we saw, an outcast by choice. Zhuangzi's writings (I will speak of them as 'his' writings for convenience, despite questions of authorship) often ridicule and undermine the implicit conformism of Confucian ethics. But they are no less subversive towards the other sort of conformism, found in the ethics of individualism. If Zhuangzi could speak to the boys in the old boarding school, he might extol them: 'Do not be a man.' An individualist, mistaking him for an ally, might join in: 'Yes, just be *yourself*!' But Zhuangzi could reply: 'No, do not be that either.' Probably he would leave the boys confused. There are many prejudices and preconceptions to overcome before his message can be properly understood. The *Zhuangzi* – the one record we have of his genius and thought – is a continual battery of fables, epigrams, riddles and jokes, aiming at breaking through the reader's defences to make room for a radical message.

The message is that true happiness and wisdom mean going *against identity*. To get there, Zhuangzi takes us into a strange and whimsical story-realm, drifting gradually away from old assumptions of who we are before arriving finally at a startlingly upside-down world. Since this effect can only be created by reading the stories directly, our own route here will have to be different. We will begin with a critique of individualism. When the falsity of individualist identity has been exposed, alongside the arbitrariness of Confucian role-based identity, then the way is cleared for Zhuangzi's radical anti-identitarian thinking.

Imagine you are living in the great dissolution of the Warring States period. Those once established as your political superiors are no longer necessarily so – their position is now openly challenged by upstarts, as identities and social order are in flux. The rites and traditions that once defined your ways of being no longer exercise absolute sovereignty. New cities have been built, with new urban elites challenging the power of those in the old regional capitals, attracting people from distant lands with strange customs. New technologies bring novel ways of farming, dressing and making war, defying older fashions and timeworn ways of life. You are much more likely to meet others in a condition of social uncertainty.

The codes of deference and duty between you and them are uncertain. Suddenly, you feel the shiver of an exciting thought. *You are free*. You are, in fact, *radically* free – free not only in your *doing* but in your *being*. Social transformation opens up fresh possibilities. You can choose, not only whether to act in accordance with your traditional political status, gender role or social station, but also whether to identify yourself by those categories.

What, then, will you be? You can, of course, return to the traditional role identity assigned to you under the old regime, as Confucius recommends. But when you try this, you find that the roles are not as they were. In the old regime there was no questioning these roles, which fully defined the individuals who entered them. Rulers were rulers. Fathers were fathers.[26] Now you are aware of an undigested portion of being that resists absorption into the role, a remainder that will not be rationalized into the cultural order. Others do not accept the traditional order, so rejection must be possible. You are able to ask: why should you accept rather than reject tradition? This makes you aware of a part of yourself that, even if it *chooses* to return to a traditional role, *could have chosen otherwise*.

In demanding that people be sincere in their roles, Confucius exposed the possibility of its opposite: a father who is only pretending to be a father, a subject who merely feigns subservience. The possibility of insincerity reveals that roles are not fully definitive. The father is a father all right, but also a musician, a person of Chu, a woodcutter, a lover of frogs . . . In a world in which new social orders are contending, rising and falling, he might have chosen to make a different one of his characteristics definitive of *his identity*. The fact that he could have chosen something else as his defining feature signals the impossibility of his ever being exhaustively defined by the choice. If he chooses to *be* a father, even in full sincerity, there is still the possibility of a different choice, and this possibility marks out the part of him that can never be fully taken into the role of fatherhood. The emergence of a sincerity regime marks the opening of an unbridgeable gulf between individual identity and the cultural order.

One possible response to the threatening possibility of choice is to revert to a sort of *primitivism* or *naturalism* – a philosophical view that nature or biology has implanted us with a true identity, lying beneath our cultural inheritance. If a chosen cultural role cannot adequately define your identity, perhaps you should look within, for an identity that nature itself has given you. Some parts of the *Zhuangzi* have been interpreted in this primitivist way: suggesting that social roles are artificial impositions and humans should go back to following their natural inclinations.[27] But this solution is not fully satisfying. Look within and what do you find? Here there might at first appear to be more solid ground: appetites, instincts, habits, character traits and other intuitions apparently fixed by nature, independent of any uncertain and dissolving cultural orders. But seizing upon these natural features in search of your identity, you realize that you are in precisely the same situation as when you strove to identify yourself with your cultural role. You can try to only follow your most natural instincts and appetites, but then you might *not* have tried this; you might, rather, have striven to overcome your innate inclinations. Since you can either surrender to or rebel against your inherent self, you and it cannot be one and the same. No less than with the social role, some part of your being resists absorption: the identification with your nature is incomplete.

Wu and Wo

What is this undigestible portion, which will not resolve into any identity? A crucial step towards an answer is taken in a famous line from the second chapter of the *Zhuangzi* (Z 2.2.1): *wu sang wo* 吾喪我, or 'I lost myself'. The crucial step is the distinction between the characters, here translated as 'I' (*wu* 吾) and 'myself' (*wo* 我).

The character *wo* 我 is an ideogram of a hand holding an axe, and has been read literally as meaning 'self-holding' or 'self-attachment'.[28] The portion of the self that is never absorbed into any identity, on the other hand, is *wu* 吾.[29] Visually, this character is composed of *wu* 五 (you can see it in the top half), which refers to the number five, but in this case might only provide the sound, and *kou* 口 (the bottom half), which represents an open mouth, perhaps indicating that *wu* 吾 stands for a way of referring to or speaking of oneself – a linguistic indexical rather than a term standing for a defined object.[30]

The *wu* 吾 is thus something that can be pointed to but never identified; it remains always beyond any objectifiable identity – that is, beyond any *wo* 我.[31] A relevant grammatical feature of *wu* 吾 is that it almost always appears in the subject position of sentences and never in the object position (it can be part of a predicate, but only when negated, e.g. 'did not see me' [*bu wu jian* 不吾見]).[32] Thus the *wu* 吾 can grasp at an idea of itself as a *wo* 我, but this idea could always change, and so in that sense our *wu* 吾 is always 'un-selfing'.[33]

One way to understand the situation of the *wu* 吾 is to compare Zhuangzi's framework to an idea presented by the nineteenth-century Danish philosopher and pioneer of existentialist philosophy, Søren Kierkegaard:

> The self wants [. . .] to savour to the full the satisfaction of making itself into itself [. . .]. And yet what it understands itself to be is in the final instance a riddle; just when it seems on the point of having the building finished, at a whim it can dissolve the whole thing into nothing.[34]

If we rewrite this passage, inserting Zhuangzi's terms, the point comes out more clearly:

> The *wu* 吾 wants to savour to the full the satisfaction of making itself into its *wo* 我. And yet what it understands its *wo* 我 to be is in the final instance a riddle; just when *wu* 吾 seems on the point of having the building finished, at a whim it can dissolve the whole thing into nothing.

Closer to our own time, in the twentieth century, some existentialist philosophers would make a grand point of this, adding (in case anyone should be tempted to relax) that deciding on your identity never ultimately settles the question of who you are. Past decisions are always revisable, so the work of choosing who to be is never finished.

For an existentialist (we will examine some sources in Chapter 7), the authentic, honest response to this situation is to sustain a constant sense of responsibility for your own being. You must never allow yourself to believe that nature, culture, heritage or circumstance have settled your identity – your *wo* 我, in Zhuangzi's terms. But there is a contradiction in the existentialist ethic.[35] Suppose that somebody does not *feel* like being authentic. If the existentialist exhorts him with a *demand* to be authentic, then this imposes authenticity as an ethical obligation. Yet authenticity imposed as an obligation seems like a contradiction in terms. The whole point of authenticity is that the *wu* 吾 *chooses* what to embrace rather than deferring to the authority of others, including even the authority of existentialist philosophers.

Existentialism is, however, only an extreme form of individualism, by which I mean the broad idea that people should determine and define their own identity. The American poet Walt Whitman's celebration of 'the thought of Identity – yours for you, whoever you are, as mine for me' explains the ideal as: 'The quality of Being, in the object's self, according to its own central idea and purpose, and of growing therefrom and thereto – not criticism by other standards, and adjustments thereto.'[36] Whitman is celebrating what he takes to be a quintessentially American form of individualism: each of us decides what and how to be, guided only by our own will and accepting no external standards besides those we choose as our own.

We may no longer celebrate it in Whitman's purple prose, but individualism is still so pervasive in modern society that we tend to underestimate its power over us.[37] Those who are presented, or present themselves, as anti-individualists are frequently merely pointing out obvious truths perfectly consistent with individualism, for example that individuals are not omnipotent and cannot determine their being independently of broader social and cultural contexts that they do not control. People who point this out are still individualists. They are sectarians peddling nuanced versions of individualism.

It does not matter which brand or level of individualism we endorse. All run into the same impasse as existentialism. The search for identity is interminable. Whatever you find or choose as your identity can always at the next moment be rejected. Culture can influence, but it does not compel. Therefore, finding or choosing your identity is never a completed task. A reasonable subject might wonder whether such an incompletable project is worth embarking on at all. But so deep has individualism sunk into our spirit that the *Zhuangzi* has to pull out every stop on the organ of rhetoric to make us even recognize the existence of options outside individualism.

Why is the search for identity interminable? It is not that the object sought, the *wo* 我 – our chosen identity – does not exist. Certainly it does not *pre*-exist in nature or culture – not, at least, once a rupture with tradition has occurred and role-based identities are thrown into question. But the *wo* 我 exists at each moment as the identity chosen by the *wu* 吾 – the innate, unknown, undefined self that is always trying to fashion itself into a chosen identity yet always remains outside it. By an ever-renewed act of choice, and subject to external influences, the *wu* 吾 builds itself into a *wo* 我: an individual with a definite identity. The process is interminable because the choice at any moment is never secure from revision by future choice. As Kierkegaard puts it, 'just when it seems on the point of having the building finished, at a whim it can dissolve the whole thing into nothing.' The construction is always revisable, and as long as it is revisable we cannot say that it is complete. You can say it is complete according to some plan you have drawn, but then the plan could always be revised as well. You can have a plan for the plan, but now you are embarked upon a regress, heading towards infinity, not finality.

What identity creation really requires is a *received* model to aim at. To be *yourself*, you need to receive and recognize some specific self to be. Individualism is really a type of conformism to a model. But how does the individual choose this model in the first instance? Must there be another exemplar to guide that choice?[38] The individualist therefore does not, despite how it might seem to her, create *any* portion of her being *ex nihilo* or in a vacuum of pure free decision.

The Transformation of Things

Nor does conforming to a model, recognized or not, ultimately solve the riddle of identity. At the end of Chapter 2 of the *Zhuangzi*, *Qiwulun* 齊物論 ('On Regarding All Things Equal') – the chapter that begins with the passage containing 'I lost myself' – is one of its most famous stories, the Butterfly Dream:

> Once Zhuang Zhou dreamt that he was a butterfly, a butterfly happy as can be, and was himself fully aware how well this suited his disposition! But he was not aware that he was Zhuang Zhou. When he awoke, he was astonished to be Zhuang Zhou, but he did not know whether he was Zhuang Zhou who had dreamt that he was a butterfly or a butterfly which was dreaming that he was Zhuang Zhou. Between Zhuang Zhou and the butterfly there had to be a boundary. And this is known as the transformation of things. (Z 2.35.1–6)

There are nearly as many interpretations of this story as there are readers. To me it beautifully illustrates how the *undefined* self, the *wu* 吾, is, as one scholar puts it, 'always un-selfing, self-fasting, or self-losing'.[39] The 'authentic self' of the *wu* 吾 is not identical to any *wo* 我. The *wu* 吾 is not defined by any identity; its being consists, rather, in not being identifiable.[40] Put bluntly, the being of the *wu* 吾 consists ultimately in *not knowing what it is*. The *wu* 吾 can grasp at various *wo* 我 to solve the enigma of the self, but these answers will only ever be provisional, always subject to revision, never ultimately satisfying.

The story ends with a recognition of *wuhua* 物化: the 'transformation of things', which is a central concept in the story.[41] It is meant to define the boundary that must exist between distinct individuals with distinct identities, such as Zhou and the butterfly. But transformation makes an odd sort of boundary. Two key notions – *self-losing* (*sangwo* 喪我) and *self-absence* (*wuwo* 無我) – are essential foundations for understanding the concept of the transformation of things.[42] When a thing transforms from 'this' into 'that', while remaining the same entity, this reveals that neither 'this' nor 'that' can be its essential identity.[43] The following chapter in the *Zhuangzi* goes on to describe the state of being *without a definite identity* (*wuwo* 無我).[44] In this state, one might take on any number of identities (*wo* 我) and yet remain fundamentally without identity, because one is not *defined* by any of these identities. Appreciating the transformation of things is to understand that things have no essential identities, including oneself.

Such appreciation means giving up on what the Japanese philosopher Toshihiko Izutsu calls the 'essentialist' view of things.[45] This is the view that each thing is what it is and not something else – 'A table is a table, for example, and it can never be a chair.'[46] According to Zhuangzi's view, this essentialist view is false. Instead, he proposes the idea of *transformism*.[47] In a transformist's view, the ontological boundaries between things are fuzzy, as the distinction between Zhou and the butterfly seems to dissolve in his dream. Things are always something else besides themselves.

Escaping Identity

The implications for identity are clear. The individual who understands transformism can escape identity, understanding that the distinctions between things are fluid and nothing ever does perfectly conform to any distinct model. Escaping identity means escaping from conformity to a model. In Guo Xiang's commentary of the *Zhuangzi*, the 'self' is taken to refer to a false notion of our identity. For the *true* self Guo typically uses a particular word, *zi* 自, which has an unusual grammatical character:[48] it also means 'self', but it can be read as an adverb rather than a noun, meaning 'spontaneously'.[49] Thus, Guo could be suggesting that the true self is not a thing at all, but a kind of spirit of spontaneity. All other kinds of self are what he calls *ji* 跡, or 'traces'.[50] *Ji* 跡 literally means 'footprints', meaning models to be imitated – ideas of the various identities that we could potentially give ourselves. Guo writes: '[One] should not follow old footsteps [. . .] He should keep himself intact and not imitate others.'[51]

Not imitating others cannot, therefore, mean *being oneself* in the individualist sense. Trying to be *like yourself* is no better than trying to be *like someone else*.[52] True non-conformism cannot be a matter of existentialist authenticity. It cannot lie in choosing your own identity and refusing to have it chosen by others or by external circumstances. To have an identity at all is necessarily to be drawn in by a model. Instead of following models and recoiling from anti-models, we must aim, as the *Zhuangzi* puts it at one point (6.10.2), to 'forget both and follow in the transformations of the Dao'. Here *dao* 道 is understood as the ever-changing way of things, mentioned above. The general flavour of the idea is nicely conveyed by a scholar of Daoist philosophy, Ellen Marie Chen (1920–2017): 'Instead of self-identity, Daoist self-transformation is a pure Dionysian intoxication with the wonderful transforming processes of Dao, at one with the butterfly, the fish, the clouds, and the elements.'[53]

What is achieved by this Daoist philosophy is a sort of elastic identity, to which scholars have given paradoxical names such as 'ironic coherence' or 'genuine pretending'.[54] To recognize that *none of the things you are defines you essentially* is to be liberated from attachment to these identities. It allows you to flow freely among them, entering into the transformation of things. For this to occur, we must achieve what the *Zhuangzi*'s sage-like character Ziqi utters to himself: *wu sang wo* 吾喪我 'I lost myself.' The *wu* 吾, the subject of this sentence, is an unselfing that rejects absorption into any *wo* 我. It achieves completion not by finding its ultimate *wo* 我, but by losing *wo* 我 (*sang wo* 喪我). Since the self never really *had* its identity, losing its identity must really mean giving up the *pursuit* of it – accepting that it will always fundamentally be *wuwo* 無我, without identity. Or, as it is put elsewhere in the *Zhuangzi* (1.7.14): *zhi ren wu ji* 至人無己: *the perfect person has no identity*.[55]

But *why* should we aim to be perfect in this way, abandoning all pursuit of identity? What if somebody accepts that the pursuit of identity is interminable, and that it involves captivation by an unchosen model, yet asserts earnestly that they find pleasure and meaning in pursuing it all the same? Why then should they give it up?

The *Zhuangzi* provides a small and a big answer to this. The small answer is that, since the pursuit of identity is really a type of model emulation, it sets off destructive cycles of rivalry, ambition and envy. This is even more dangerous when it occurs unconsciously – when we believe ourselves to be individualists and overlook the fact that we are really emulating models. A great deal of human violence and cruelty stems from these egotistical dynamics, so it seems hardly a small matter. But it is minor when compared to the bigger picture. The main answer is that the pursuit of identity runs against the very grain of existence. To fight it is to doom yourself to endless frustration, and, in fact, to turn your life into a sort of living death.

2.

Avoid Footprints

The Self-Portrait

Timothy Mo's novel *An Insular Possession* contains a powerful statement of the doctrine of *metaphysical desire* – the theory that our sense of identity determines everything we do:

> Men will not act by grand plans or formulations of a scheme of ideas, or even by the implication of a vested interest, but in the very first instance by the notion they entertain of themselves – and this picture they draw of their private characters is one to which they will address themselves with assiduity of purpose over many years.[1]

The speaker of these words is a painter named Harry O'Rourke. Although driven by appetites – strongly disposed towards wine, food and younger female subjects – O'Rourke is vain and sensitive to the slightest insult to his pride. When another character acquires a camera and begins a career in pioneering photography, Harry feels threatened and becomes embroiled in an endless argument over whether painting or photography is the superior visual art. The metaphor is clear: the characters are competing over self-portraits. Harry is driven in all he does by the picture he draws of himself and the striving for it to be what others see in him.[2] This tendency leads to squabbles; the narrative sizzles with snubs, insults, acrimonies and duels.

This theme runs not only in the foreground action but also in the book's historical background: the escalation of the First Opium War, fought in 1839–42 between the Qing dynasty ruling China and the British Empire, which aimed at maintaining its 'right' to sell narcotics in China in order to maintain its balance of trade. Mo's novel follows a group of employees of a US trading company, some of whom take a principled stand against their employer's entry into the opium trade and one of whom learns Chinese to gain a unique perspective on the conflict. Just before the passage quoted, this figure observes how the ruling Qing mandarins refuse in their writing 'to elevate the character for Queen Victoria one line above the other characters in the same sentence, as they would for "Emperor" '.[3] The British identify themselves as a great empire led by a great queen, one whose name is to be elevated at least as high as that of any other earthly sovereign. The mandarins, knowing full well that the British regard them as inferior savages, are in no way disposed to symbolically elevate those who denigrate them. History is driven by the inflexible notions that these nations entertain of themselves and the threats they pose to each other's sense of pride and self-worth. Insults compound, the battle for status cannot be contained by diplomacy, and eventually we see iron-sided gunboats steaming up the Canton River.[4]

All these characters require that their identity – and that of their nation – be recognized and emulated by others. Imitation would be the sincerest form of flattery, gratifying their thirst for glory. The problem, as ever, is that each side wants to be the emulated, not the emulator, even as they unconsciously mimic each other's growing sense of pride and aggression. We saw, in the previous chapter, that the *Zhuangzi* starts with the

Confucian premise that the way towards identity is to imitate an exemplar. But it moves on from this tradition – and in this chapter we shall trace how it steps out from this idea.

Footprints

As we have seen, the ethical system of the ancient Zhou was fundamentally based on emulation.[5] This tradition has a long, ongoing influence over Chinese political philosophy. For example, during the Cultural Revolution of the 1960s and 70s, even while Confucian tradition was explicitly rejected, the novelist Yu Hua recalls how the emulation of admirable exemplars played a potent ideological role: 'Everyone scrutinized his own thinking for inequalities, for gaps between himself and progressive individuals like the exemplary soldier Lei Feng. "Study advanced models, note disparities" – such was the catchphrase of the day.'[6] The quotation is from Chairman Mao, but it would not be out of place in Confucius's *Analects*.

The *Zhuangzi* strongly opposes this imitative ethics, and it delivers this message through the image of footprints. The image of 'footprints' (*ji* 跡) comes from Guo's commentary rather than Zhuangzi, but Guo invokes it in order to emphasize the anti-imitation themes of the main text. For example, Guo comments on one passage – 'Therefore alas do not benevolence and righteousness belong to one's innate character' (Z 8.4.4–5) – by noting that people have abandoned their natures in order to 'chase after the footprints' of others, and this has 'resulted in much grief'.[7] The criticism here is of the exemplarist ethics, which leads people to seek virtues – benevolence and righteousness – in the imitation of models instead of in their own nature. In pursuing an exemplary identity, we are led into contention and grief.

But do not be misled into thinking that Zhuangzi's term 'innate character' (情) or Guo's term 'nature' (*xing* 性) refers to some definite innate identity. The point, rather, is to problematize the whole process of self-definition by way of a model. There are several problems with the pursuit of identity models, or footprints, as Guo calls them.

First, imitation binds us to our models and hinders our adaptability to circumstances for which it is not appropriate.[8] As Guo puts it: 'Devotion to footprints already made as a means to control the infinitely changeable is such that when the infinitely changeable arrives, to follow these footprints is sure to get one bogged down' (Z 10.2.1).

Next, imitation gives rise to what Guo refers to (Z 5.31) as 'impossible envy'. When we imitate a model, we want to be the model, not the imitator. Yet in fact we are the imitator, not the model. We are striving to be like our model, but is that something our model would do?[9] Guo denies (Z 5.31) that the sages and worthies were imitators of models, telling us that they themselves had no predilection to *try to be* sages and worthies. Thus, in imitating them we actually mark our difference from them. Even if Guo is wrong and the sages *are* imitators, we are unlikely to become such popular exemplars as they are. We will never have the prestige of those we emulate. Our emulation will always be incomplete and unsatisfying. Our exemplars will become objects of impossible envy.

Finally, imitation is harmful.[10] Guo provides a striking commentary on a passage in which the *Zhuangzi* asserts that it is no use trying to emulate a list of sages. The commentary is:

> All these were endowed with so much versatility that they made everyone in the world dance after them in emulation, but in emulating them, people lost what they themselves were.

> It was this loss of self due to them that made them masters of chaos, and the great disaster that has so afflicted the world is caused by just this loss of self. (Z 10.5.12)

On Not Being Like Yourself

It is a mistake to identify Zhuangzi's project with the pursuit of *authenticity* celebrated in much Western philosophy.[11] The *Zhuangzi* does not advise us to give up imitating others only to recommend that we instead find our *true self*, our *real identity*. It reminds us that trying to be like yourself is no better than trying to be like somebody else.[12]

Guo, in his commentary on the *Zhuangzi*, strongly criticizes the pursuit of *youwei* 有為 – or 'selfconscious purpose' (2.14.25).[13] *Youwei* 有為 is the opposite of *wuwei* 無為, which we have seen previously to mean 'non-action'. *You* 有 means to have, to exist, to possess, presence. *Wu* 無 means to negate, nothing, naught. *Wei* 為 means to do, to become and to make, but also *to identify*.[14] Thus, Guo makes clear that the goal is *not* to deliberately pursue some authentic notion of the self and whatever goals that notion defines. Rather, it means trying not to be led by goals, ambitions or a notion of self at all.

In this case, Guo is suggesting that searching for your identity leads you not to your fundamental nature but instead to 'endlessly seek outside it to become something else' (Z 2.14.25). When Guo refers to our *benxing* 本性, fundamental nature, and Zhuangzi refers to our *qing* 情, innate character, these should therefore be taken not as referring to any defined identity but rather to the self as *wu* 吾. As we have seen, *wu* 吾 stands for a sort of self that is more like an *unselfing*.[15] This would explain why acting with *self-conscious* knowledge, *youwei* 有為, really means losing your fundamental nature. *Youwei* 有為 could mean deeming yourself under a specific identity – a *wo* 我 – and thus losing sight of the undetermined, identityless nature of your *wu* 吾.

What would it then be to act *without* an identity as a defining goal – to practise *wuwei* 無為? An important passage in Guo's commentary is where it describes the mindset of the sage:

> [The sage] merges with Heaven and Earth and with the innate tendencies of perfect principle. When this involves things that he himself must ponder, it is not that he ponders them with a personal self, and when this involves things that he himself must not ponder, it is not that he refrains from pondering them with a personal self either. Sometimes he ponders and so avoids something, sometimes he ponders and does not avoid something, sometimes he does not ponder and yet avoids something, and sometimes he does not ponder and yet does not avoid something. In all these cases it is not his personal self that is responsible for anything, so what more should he do? He just lets things spontaneously fulfil themselves. (Z 5.28.8)

The ideal presented here is one of letting things happen spontaneously, inside and outside yourself, without thinking about *what you are trying to become* in doing so. The sage's unselfconscious way of being is not inactive, nor is it unthinking. What is distinctive about the true sage is a lack of *egotism*. When the sage does things, it is not 'with a personal self', not with a *wo* 我. The sage breaks Harry O'Rourke's law that: 'Men act [. . .] in the very first instance by the notion they entertain of themselves.'

Free of egotistical motivations, sages are unbothered when 'pondering' – strategizing – fails to help them to avoid evils.

Often our misery at misfortune is driven at least in part by our wounded pride at *being somebody who failed* to master circumstances. Sages have no pride to wound. They can try to achieve things in the world, but not to *be* a certain sort of character, nor to take pride in *being* competent or masterful. They simply do not act with a personal self at all; they do not *wei* 為 in its dual senses of 'identity' and 'act with purpose'. They have no egotistical need to master circumstances and can adapt when their exploratory ventures fail.[16]

The Gardener: Glory

The *Zhuangzi* continues its anti-authenticity attitude through the story of the gardener (Z 12.25–34), which appears in Chapter 12, *Tiandi* 天地 ('Heaven and Earth') – one of the so-called 'outer chapters', which are less likely than the first seven to have been written by Zhuang Zhou. A character named Zigong, a philosophical searcher and disciple of Confucius, encounters a gardener carrying a jug from a well to water his plants and instructs him on how to build a simple pump that 'in one day can irrigate a hundred gardens'. The gardener surprises Zigong by replying that while he knows about such machines, he refuses to use them, because someone who uses them has 'a machine-like mind', is 'impaired in his pure simplicity', and has an unstable spiritual life, not supported by the Dao.[17]

After Zigong admits that he is a follower of Confucius, the gardener continues the attack, accusing Zigong of being 'one of those who broaden their learning so as to appear like the sages, fawn and flatter so to rise above the masses, strumming and singing sad solos so to peddle their reputations to the world!' And he advises him: 'Would that you soon forget your spirit, discard your body, and perhaps then you might get close to it' – in other words, lose yourself to find yourself. Zigong is deeply chastened and rethinks his whole ethical position (Z 12.33.1–3). He feels he has found in the gardener the ethic of *wuwei* 無為 – the anti-egotistical rejection of conscious ambitions in favour of spontaneous flowing along. The gardener might represent one aspect of Daoism: a sort of primitivism that rejects all the achievements and ambitions associated with human civilization.

But when Zigong tells Confucius about the gardener, Confucius sees through the gardener's self-righteous stance. He tells Zigong that the gardener is attempting to cultivate the techniques of Hundun – presumably to recover his innocent, 'uncarved' quality. But the attempt fails. Confucius tells Zigong:

> Someone who attains natural simplicity through brightness and clarity, recovers pristine simplicity through unselfconscious action, and safeguards his spirit through embodiment of original nature, and [. . .] thanks to all that can wander freely throughout the common world. (Z 12.34.1–4)

The gardener, Confucius is implying, does not match this description. He does not 'wander freely through the common world', and this belies his self-presentation as somebody with 'natural simplicity'.

Guo's commentary helps to explain Confucius's response to the gardener by adding to it: 'though [someone who really attains natural simplicity] merges with the waves of the world, he never violates who he really is (*zishi* [自是]), and, though he wanders freely throughout the common world, he is so completely one with it that he leaves no footprints in it.'

What Confucius has noticed is that the gardener's preaching does not match his practice. The gardener preaches the forgetting of the spirit. He chastises Zigong for seeking to rise above the masses and peddle his reputation. His rejection of machinery could be viewed as a metaphor for avoiding emulation: the gardener does not want to become like an external thing or develop an imitative 'machine-like mind'. And yet, Confucius notices, the way that he flaunts his authenticity and lords it over Zigong shows that he is far from the Hundunian ideal of self-forgetting. The gardener's boastfulness demonstrates that he has not forgotten himself at all. 'One who boasts about himself has no merit', as a later chapter, quoting the *Daodejing*, puts it (Z 20.16.8).[18] The gardener in fact shows an attitude of ambition towards Zigong – an attempt to influence him through criticism, to make Zigong *more like himself*, or at least to glory in his superiority. The gardener treads hard on the world and leaves footprints. He does not wander freely through the world and merge with its waves.

The Vanishing and Faceless Sage

The gardener's attitude is in stark contrast to the sage celebrated by Confucius, who, according to Guo's elaboration, 'lets achievements and honors revert to the natural usefulness of all and arcanely merges with others – thus leaving no footprints of his own' (Z 4.44.4). 'Leaving no footprints of his own' seems to mean neither influencing others nor seeking to influence them. Guo goes on to say: 'To take something of your own and try to rule others with it now means that you will fail to merge arcanely with others'

(Z 4.45.7). A different translation reads: 'If one possesses a self (*you ji* 有己) and faces objects [with it], one cannot vanish (into) things.'[19] The phrase *you ji* 有己, 'possessing a self', is a direct contrast to the message of the *Zhuangzi*, which I highlighted earlier: *zhi ren wu ji* 至人無己 – 'the perfect person has no identity' (Z 1.7.14) – here 'no identity' translates as *wu ji* 無己, which is the direct antonym of *you ji* 有己 (*ji* 己 can be translated as 'self' or 'identity'). Guo seems to be saying that *having an identity* – a conscious notion of self – prevents one from deeply connecting with others. It is impossible to be driven by a picture of yourself without wanting others to flatter and affirm that picture by imitation. Thus, Confucius observes how the gardener has not at all succeeded in cultivating the techniques of Hundun.[20]

The passage quoted above (Z 4.45.7) suggests that to be *truly* Hundun-like would be to 'merge arcanely with others' – or 'vanish (into) things' in the alternative translation quoted. Elsewhere, Guo points out that Hundun 'arcanely unites' with things (Z 12.34.5). Terms like 'merge arcanely' and 'unite arcanely' appear often in Guo's commentary, sometimes translating as *xuantong* 玄同 (literally 'dark unity')[21] and sometimes *ming* 冥, which, as one translator of the *Zhuangzi*, Brook Ziporyn points out, means 'dark' but is often used by Guo as a verb.[22] To *ming* 冥 into others is to lose your identity in them, which perhaps means to encounter others without the interaction being governed by some notion of your own and their identity.[23] At one point Guo writes: 'Freedom from the "other" and "this one" is how one achieves arcane unity' (Z 2.10.1). In the condition of arcane unity, you no longer think of yourself in relation to others but are so submerged in the interaction that you no longer identify its distinct participants. When Guo warns about footprints leading us away from our *true self*, he is not referring to a true authentic identity. Instead, he points to pure spontaneity – the very *absence* of any notion of your own identity – the facelessness of Hundun or the unselfing of the *wu* 吾.

What reveals the gardener to be a false sage is that he is taken with a certain idea of himself. He *identifies* himself in contrast with, and as superior to, Zigong. He studies advanced models and notes discrepancies. As a result, his encounter with Zigong is hostile. A true sage would never have such a hostile encounter. True sages *ming* 冥 into others with no sense of themselves at all. They practise unselfconscious action, *wuwei* 無為, and esteem neither themselves (as identified in some specific way) nor others. Many passages from Guo's commentary bear this out:

> One perfectly content realizes that comings and goings depend not on the person he himself is. Therefore, there is nothing for him to invest either humility or arrogance in. (Z 2.14.18)
>
> To regard oneself as right and the other wrong, to esteem oneself and despise the other, from those of middling intelligence on down to insects, all without exception behave like this. But this is to understand just themselves and fail to understand others. However, those who arcanely interchange and merge imperceptibly with things understand the whole world from the point of view of the whole world. (Z 5.6.2)
>
> The surge of desire never fails to make people denigrate the less and esteem the more, so when they see something they so envy [in others], they work themselves up to augment it [in themselves], and by trying to aggrandize their fundamental functions, they distress the original nature they have by nature. But if they would forget about what they esteem and instead safeguard their own fundamental allotted capacity, then, free

> of anything extraneous to their original natures, all their various measures would remain whole and safe. (Z 8.1.5)

A true sage would thank Zigong for his advice and then allow her own spontaneous whim to follow it or not. She would *not* think about whether following Zigong's advice would make her into somebody with a 'machine-like heart'. She would not think at all about *what sort of being* different courses of action would mark her out as. She would be moved by curious delight in other things – thus vanishing into them – and not by any picture drawn of her private character.

This is why Confucius says: 'Someone who attains natural simplicity through brightness and clarity', who 'recovers pristine simplicity through unselfconscious action, and safeguards his spirit through embodiment of original nature' is able to 'wander freely throughout the common world'. Such a person has no problem in taking advice or following along with local customs. Pride does not get in the way, and there is no ambitious drive to display superior or independent status.

Identity and Violence

Zigong's encounter with the gardener is acrimonious but not violent. Yet it reveals how identity, and all the manoeuvres of pride and egotism it sets off, can lead towards hostility. We can imagine the interaction having gone quite differently if Zigong had felt less submissively inferior. Imagine if, for example, he was spurred to defend his Confucian identity against the disrespect of the gardener. When two ambitious individuals meet, each insists on influencing the other (having their identity affirmed) yet not being influenced (surrendering their identity). There is no equilibrium. This is the real danger of *youwei* 有為, self-conscious action, driven by an inner emulative model of the ideal self or what the *Zhuangzi* calls a footprint. Footprints lead into the paths of other heavy-treaders.

The connection between identity and conflict is strong but subtle. A modern illustration can be found in the twentieth-century author V. S. Naipaul's travelogue of some parts of the Islamic world, *Among the Believers*. At one point, Naipaul records his admonishment to a Malay villager who was educated at a mission school, which the villager calls 'Christian and secular'. Naipaul adds that 'secular was the bad word with these men: it meant worldly, atheistic, western, non-Malay'. Through this alienating education, the villager has lost his sense of self. But Naipaul replies: 'In what way were you confused? My background is more complicated than yours, but I am not confused.'[24] Naipaul, a Trinidadian of Indian descent, educated in a British school and then Oxford University, is not confused by his background. But then Naipaul is a famous author, celebrated around the world and destined for a Nobel Prize. That is to say, *who he is* is celebrated and affirmed around the world. It is not the site of any obvious conflict, inner or outer. But who are the men he is speaking with? Low-status migrant workers – interchangeable units of labour in the eyes of the urban elites, amputees from the social body of their former villages. It is hardly a puzzle why Naipaul should feel confident in his identity while they feel lost and insecure.

Naipaul's confidence, nevertheless, might seem to challenge the warnings about footprints in Guo's commentary. He appears to succeed in trying to be himself, without frustration or danger. But we can look deeper. Why is Naipaul so hard on the villagers and many other decolonized, identity-challenged people he sometimes disparages as 'mimic men' – mere imitators?[25] A contemporary theorist of global conflict, Pankaj Mishra, notes how Naipaul himself 'succumbed to the pathology of mimic machismo he had once feared and despised' by supporting Hindu nationalist movements later in his life, even when they committed atrocities against Muslims.[26] Perhaps the roots of this attitude can already be seen in the dialogue with the villagers. Naipaul has few kind words to say about Islam throughout *Among the Believers* and its sequel *Beyond Belief*.[27] Islam, perhaps, appears as a challenge to his own Indian heritage, a part of India's cultural history that is not reflected in his own background. His Indian heritage, meanwhile, is part of what marks him out against a '"savourless" and "mean" life in England' (Mishra takes these words from Naipaul himself).[28] And so perhaps his identity is not so confident and unconfused after all. Perhaps the insecurity around it – just as Guo would predict – leads to an endorsement of violence. Naipaul's unkindness to the villagers is like the gardener's arrogance towards Zigong. It is born of a pursuit of identity that can never be fully secure. Naipaul might not be confused. The gardener might not have a machine-like heart. But they are, all the same, more troubled than they realize.

Mishra makes these comments about Naipaul in a book that studies how notions of identity lead people into conflict, or at least to celebrate it. In another example, he reminds us that the perpetrator of a brutal massacre in Orlando, Florida in 2016, generally regarded as an act of Islamic terrorism, 'could not tell the difference between such bitterly opposed groups as ISIS, al-Qaeda, and Hezbollah' and that 'his most significant ideological act during his killing spree was checking his Facebook pages and Googling himself'.[29] It was not Islam that moved him. It was his sense of himself as a heroic jihadi. Islam, at least some distorted projection of it, featured in the picture he drew of his private character. But it was not a picture of Islam. It was a self-portrait. Likewise, when a white-nationalist mass shooter murdered fifty people at a mosque in Christchurch, New Zealand, the prime minister made the decision to deny him the notoriety he sought by refusing to mention his name.[30] She recognized him as a man intent on elevating not just his race but himself in particular.

And when Black Lives Matter protestors toppled the statue of the slave trader Edward Colston in Bristol, organizations such as Britain First and the Democratic Football Lads Alliance (real name) sent crowds to guard other statues deemed to be under threat. Why travel for miles to protect a statue you would most likely never have looked at otherwise, which is far from being an artistic masterpiece? Perhaps the statues signified to these counter-protestors something bound up with their feelings of self: a picture of Britain, or the history they were taught in school, which had become a crucial background to their inner self-portraits. The British essayist Emily Bootle writes: 'One of the protestors told the *Daily Mail*: "I'm here purely to protect our history." In reality, it is hard not to infer that he was trying to protect his sense of self.'[31] She explains: 'You cannot be who you are – British – unless Britain looks like you.'[32] And so: 'More often than not, culture wars are started when who *you* are appears to challenge someone else's sense of who *they* are.'[33]

Identity does not necessarily lead to conflict and violence. But Zhuangzi exposes why it does so often, and why it is always something to be feared. He also presents it as grounded in a fundamentally mistaken view of the ultimate nature of reality.

3.
Nothing in Particular

Human Identity

Zhuangzi's recommendation as we have presented it so far is that we should avoid the pursuit of identity altogether. We should avoid *youwei* 有為, or self-conscious action. But we have seen how radical a proposal this is. How can I consciously aim at financial success, or living an ethical life, or supporting my family without working with some image, however vague, of *myself* as a financial success, ethical agent or family man? If Zhuangzi is telling us to give up on all such dreams, ambitions and life projects, he had better have a very good reason. Do the dangers of identity constitute a strong enough rationale?

It is tempting to reach for a more moderate response to these dangers. One alternative is articulated by contemporary philosophers Kwame Anthony Appiah and Amartya Sen. While they know well the dangers of identity, they propose that we should not give up on it altogether. Instead, we should pursue broader and more inclusive notions of identity. Appiah calls on us to embrace the most general possible identity as 'an identity that should bind us all'.[1] He finds the expression of this in a line by the Roman poet Publius Terentius Afer, known as Terence: 'I think nothing human alien to me.' He notes how Terence himself was a great many things: from humble origins as a slave in Carthage, North Africa, he rose, after being freed, to become celebrated for his commentaries on Greek comedies and even to hold a seat in the Senate. He balanced literary and political life and continued to call himself an African while celebrating his Roman identity.[2]

Sen meanwhile takes inspiration from the title character in a novel, *Gora*, by his fellow Bengali, Rabindranath Tagore. Gora begins as a staunch Hindu conservative and then, when it emerges that he is in fact the adopted child of Irish parents ('Gora' means fair-skinned), 'finds all the doors of traditionalist temples closed to him – as a "foreign-born" – thanks to the narrowly conservative cause which he himself had been championing'.[3] As Sen reads the novel, what Gora achieves at the end is 'to see himself just as a human being who is at home in India, not delineated by religion or caste or class or complexion'.[4]

These exemplars, at least as Appiah and Sen see them, do not escape identity. They retain expansive identities – identities defined in terms of inclusion rather than exclusion, in terms of rejecting the importance of religion, caste, class and complexion.

Yet such identities can still lead to insecurity, strife and violence. Those who claim to see themselves as 'just human' can be very hard on those who find their identity in something more specific. Those who emulate John Lennon's 'no religion' can take an attitude of mocking superiority to those who identify themselves by their faith. Cosmopolitans who shun ethnic identity can excoriate the bigotry of others, yet in doing so they often reveal that they are fighting their own insecurity by chasing a superior social status among a certain cosmopolitan crowd.[5]

An identity built upon a commitment to broad inclusion can still lead to egotism, competition, groupishness and glory-seeking. Like Zhuangzi's gardener, someone who takes on such a moral identity with the best of intentions can end up lording it over others as much as any high-flying investment banker or fraternity bully. Battles for status can break out among the supporters of tolerance and inclusivity – over what those core values really mean and how best to have them, and (what is more often the issue) over who most truly and authentically cares about them – who sits at the high table in the College of the Just. Even the footprints of Terence can lead to the dangers of vainglory and rivalry.

As for Gora, I am not sure that Sen has him quite right. Right at the start of the novel, Tagore quotes a song:

> In and out the cage, how the unknown bird doth flit;
> I'd chain it with my heart, if I could but capture it.[6]

Might Tagore be giving us a clue here? Might the *unknown* bird represent a being beyond identity, impossible to be captured by the mind under any particular concept? In one of his philosophical writings, Tagore writes that: 'Joy is the outcome of detachment from self and lives in freedom of spirit.'[7] And in an unpublished poem, he writes:

> This pride of name plucks feathers from others to decorate its own self and to drown all other music it beats its own drum. Oh, let it be utterly defeated in me and let the day come when only thy name will play in my tongue and I shall be accepted by all by my nameless recognition.[8]

Perhaps what Gora achieves is not a more expansive and tolerant self – a *merely human* identity – but an escape from identity altogether. Rather than learning 'to see himself just as a human being who is at home in India', perhaps Gora finds himself at home – vanishing into things – because he has stopped seeing himself as anything, or seeing himself at all, or even wanting to be seen and recognized. Like the unknown bird, he flits in and out of the cage of distinct selfhood. He finds himself accepted in his nameless recognition.

Tagore might believe, as Zhuangzi seems to, that pursuing a broader identity is not enough for true happiness. For that, identity must be rejected altogether. But, setting aside the many dangers of identity, why would abandoning it be necessary for true happiness?

Things Are Not What They Are

Consider, first, why Appiah and Sen are unable to take the step of rejecting identity wholesale. Perhaps they are stuck within a broadly Aristotelian paradigm. Aristotle (384–322 BCE), the ancient Greek philosopher who exerted an unrivalled influence on the three great Abrahamic faiths,[9] is often held up as a mascot of identity-based thinking. For instance, in *Selfie: How the West Became Self-Obsessed*, British journalist Will Storr tells of his experience on a course at the Esalen Institute, ground zero of the US self-help movement. The course leader, the film actress Paula Shaw, begins by outlining three rules. '[T]he first one goes back to Aristotle: a thing is what it is.' Storr continues the story:

> She stood and lifted her seat in front of her. 'This is a chair. It has a plastic back and metal legs. It has certain properties, weight, height, depth. It is what it is. Got it? OK. Rule number two: own it. Rule number three: be creative with it.' She sat

back down and grinned. 'I hope you're ready. Because we're going to light a firecracker under you.'[10]

Aristotle is invoked by Shaw as articulating a basic principle of identity – *a thing is what it is* – undergirding a quest for self-discovery, or self-expansion, or anyway self-*something*. This is *youwei* 有為 to a Californian extreme. The first step in this self-promotional journey is knowing that things are what they are. Each thing has its identity, and that includes you. Own it.

The contrast between Aristotelian and early Daoist thinking on this point has been studied by Ellen Chen. Aristotelian thinking, she proposes, endorses a 'form motive': 'By becoming a fixed form immune to change and dissolution, finite individuals hope to escape swallowing by the Infinite.'[11] Putting it less extremely, the individual driven by the form motive seeks to achieve and preserve a certain fixed identity, to avoid dissolving into undefinition or becoming a *nobody*. By contrast, Daoism endorses a 'matter motive', according to which 'a living universe is one wherein the many finite forms are ever coalescing, interpenetrating, appearing and disappearing'.[12] In effect, the message is: do not worry about not being what *you* are; *nothing, in fact, is what it is*. In other words, Shaw's first rule is false.[13]

Those driven by the form motive are haunted by the sentiment so well expressed by Oscar Wilde: 'Most people are other people. Their thoughts are someone else's opinions, their lives a mimicry, their passions a quotation.'[14] This mimicry is blamed for violating the Aristotelian law of identity. A chair is what it is and not something else, so why do people find it so difficult to be who they are and not somebody else? Here, analytic philosophers might flap their wings at the confusion between two different senses of identity (they apply the form motive to meanings as well). But Zhuangzi's response would be to sphinxishly ask if we are so sure that the chair is a chair at all.

In Chapter 1, I referred to Zhuangzi's *transformism*, which contrasts with the Aristotelian view, there called *essentialism*. The essentialist view holds that things are what they are and not something else: 'A table is a table, for example, and it can never be a chair,' as Izutsu puts it.[15] Zhuangzi, however, 'is convinced that [this] is *not* the ultimate view of things'. In his alternative view, *transformism*, things 'lose their solidity, and become liquified', and we lose sight of 'any marked distinction to be drawn between a table and a chair, between a table and a book'. As a result: 'Everything is itself and yet, at the same time, all other things.' Or, put otherwise: 'all things interpenetrate each other and transform themselves into one another endlessly. All things are "one" – in a dynamic way.'[16]

The central notion of *transformation* (*hua* 化) means something much broader than mere change. It is applied to the story of the butterfly dream, discussed in Chapter 1, where Zhuang Zhou does not *change* into a butterfly but merely *dreams* he is one. The dream is no mere fantasy; it reveals an aspect of reality in which Zhou *is* a butterfly.

Of course, this claim needs justifying and explaining. But note first that breaking the first of Shaw's rules moves us away from the way of the *self*, marked out so lucratively at Esalen. Suppose that things are not so distinct and demarcated as we think. Suppose that they are not so straightforwardly *what they are*. As a contrast to the world of identities and essences, Zhuangzi depicts a world of transformation, indistinctness and irreducible ambiguity. To give up on the pursuit of identity would then be to make peace with such a world. To try to hold onto identity in the face of it would be to commit yourself to a doomed mission.

There Is No One Who Is Not Another

Chapter 2 of the *Zhuangzi*, *Qiwulun* 齊物論 ('On Regarding All Things Equal'), presents a sustained attack on essentialism. This is conveyed strongly in passages such as:

> There is no one who is not an 'other'; there is no one who is not a 'this one'. If it is from the point of view of the other, then one does not see it; if it is from what oneself knows, then one knows it. (Z 2.10.1)

The terms translated as 'this one' and 'other' are *shi* 是 and *bi* 彼. *Shi* 是, 'this', is a demonstrative, which picks out a distinct thing.[17] But the distinctions that demonstrative terms make, between *this* and *that*, *self* and *other*, *here* and *there*, are indexed to your point of view. For me to point out one thing to you, marking it out from others, you and I need to share a common point of view. If, for instance, I want to point out a star in the sky, you have to move close enough to me to view the sky from my perspective.

Later Zhuangzi adds: ' "What is" depends for its existence on "what is not", and "what is not" depends for its existence on "what is" ' (Z 2.10.3). Referencing a logical riddle well known in his time,[18] Zhuangzi goes on to hint that by drawing on this notion we can show that a horse is not a horse.[19] What counts as a horse from one perspective does not count from another. It matters what we want horses for, what we are comparing them to. There is always the possibility of alternative perspectives from which this creature would not be deemed a horse. We can imagine a strict naturalist who believes that a horse is a wild animal of the plains, and a yoked and saddled beast like this one is a human corruption, a travesty of a horse (a later chapter in the *Zhuangzi* comes close to suggesting this) (Z 9.4.1–2). We can suppose a culture that uses large horses for transport and small horses as pets and therefore develops no single category of 'horse'. We can imagine perspectives from which our separation of horses from non-horses makes no sense or is made in a different way. The very fact that we can deem something to be a certain way from our perspective entails the possibility of other perspectives from which it can be deemed not to be that way.[20] By deeming a thing one way, we touch the possibility of deeming it another way.[21]

The view, in other words, is that things are as they are as a matter of convention,[22] and conventions differ and give different results depending on how and where they are applied (Z 2.11.3–5). From this, Zhuangzi draws the moral: 'Therefore, the sage follows not such a path but instead illuminates things with the light of Heaven and indeed depends on this' (Z 2.10.4). The path avoided by the sage is that of *saying what things are*, from a given perspective. Guo comments: 'To stay perfectly unbiased means following the "what is" and "what is not" of the whole world so that one stays free of any "what is" and "what is not" of one's own' (Z 2.10.4). Since 'what is' and 'what is not' differs among perspectives, accepting this perspectival nature of things, while 'staying free of any "what is" and "what is not" of one's own', must mean resisting the temptation to mistake the way things are from your own perspective as the way they are absolutely.

Zhuangzi gives further examples (Z 2.11.6). Standing

upright, a crossbeam is horizontal and the pillar vertical; lying sideways the pillar is horizontal and the crossbeam vertical. By conventional standards, a leper is ugly and the famous beauty Xi Shi is beautiful; by other standards it would be the reverse. In saying that 'the Dao treats them as one and the same', I believe Zhuangzi to be saying that at the ultimate level – from the perspective of the Dao – things are both ways. They have the potential to be taken in this or that way from various perspectives. And so the Aristotelian dictum that *a thing is what it is* requires revision.

Take Shaw's chair. She tells us: 'It has certain properties, weight, height, depth.' But what these are depends on who you ask. It might be heavy for me and light for a professional furniture mover, small to me and big to a child. As Zhuangzi puts it: 'In the whole world nothing is any larger than the tip of an autumn hair, yet Mount Tai is small, and no one is more long-lived than a dead infant, yet Pengzu [a legendary figure who lived for 450 years] died young' (Z 2.13.12). The passage is mysterious, yet Zhuangzi seems to be thinking about the relativity of 'large', 'small', 'old' and 'young', among other things.[23]

You might be tempted to reply that, yes, *these* qualities are in the eye of the beholder, but there are objective measures of weight (or at least mass), height and depth – 18 kilograms, 150 centimetres, etc. As it happens, these are not absolute either.[24] If an object moves past us very fast, its length along the axis of its motion is compressed and its mass is increased, compared with when it is at rest. But, of course, it *is* at rest as viewed from an object moving alongside it at the same speed. We must look much deeper than size and mass if we hope to find quantities not relative to a frame of reference. I am not saying that there are no such qualities, nor that Zhuangzi would say this.

I propose that Zhuangzi is not explicit about how thoroughgoing his relativism is because this is not his main lesson.[25] His point is that the properties that ordinary people find in things *often* turn out to be merely relative, and we cannot always predict when this will turn out to be the case. When we reflect properly, we often find that things which appeared *absolutely* to be a certain way in fact only appear that way from our point of view. So who are we to insist that our point of view reveals the absolute truth? The sage, illuminating things in the light of Heaven, does not.

Off the Road of Right and Wrong

Zhuangzi's transformism applies most readily to the *values* of things. When Zhuangzi uses terms like 'so' (*ran* 然) and 'suitable' (*ke* 可), he might mean these as value judgements, meaning *correct*, *worthy*, *good*, etc. Then Zhuangzi's statement that 'no thing fails to be "so"; no thing fails to be "suitable"' suggests that, since things are only 'so' and 'suitable' by being deemed as such, everything in itself is both so and not so, having the potential to be deemed both ways. Thus, the Aristotelian law does not apply to values: a thing (from one perspective) is *not* what it is (from another), when we mean by 'what it is' something like good, bad, worthy or unworthy, for example. Thus, Zhuangzi concludes that 'the sage does not walk along the road of right and wrong'.[26]

This sort of value-perspectivism has some bad associations. Coming back to the present day, Appiah gives examples of how it is worryingly easy to use perspectivism to justify anything, for instance 'ASEAN[27] despots [. . .] arguing that human rights campaigns are just another colonial attempt to impose Western norms upon "Asian values"', or 'those who defend the infibulation ("Pharaonic circumcision") of female offspring as an expression of "African values"'.[28] But his examples should not lead us to worry about Zhuangzi's position. ASEAN despots using relativist justifications for their oppression cannot claim a more solid basis in Zhuangzi's transformism than Western colonialists.

President Suharto of Indonesia exercised despotism in part by failing to acknowledge perspectives *within Indonesia* from which values did not line up with his Pancasila programme, or which interpreted '*Pancasila*' differently (more on this in Chapter 7). Appiah also makes the important observation that failures of understanding 'can occur just as easily with narratives and neighborhoods around the corner as they do with those from far away'.[29] Likewise, practices of genital mutilation survive in part through blindness towards any *local* perspective from which they appear wrong, as sensitively represented in Ousmane Sembène's 2004 film *Moolaadé*.

Zhuangzi does not advance perspectivism as an ideological weapon, to justify pushing away rivals to one's own perspective on the grounds of resistance to colonial imposition. He advances it as a therapeutic instrument for loosening the attachment to your own perspective, which is what drove you to see other perspectives as rivals in the first place (it is also what allows colonists to dismiss all doubts about their claims to superiority).[30] His purpose is not to insulate us within our own relative perspectives, but to *ming* 冥 – 'arcanely merge' – perspectives into each other.[31] The lesson of perspectivism is not that we can justify our own perspective as valid relative to itself; it is that we should attain an open heart.

The Pivot of the Dao

Put otherwise, Zhuangzi's transformism calls us to venture not *deeper into our own perspective* but away from it, towards what he calls the 'pivot of the Dao' (*dao shu* 道樞).[32] This is the point at the centre of all perspectives, from which we recognize the possibility of infinitely many ways of grasping and valuing things (Z 12.10.9–11). The *dao shu* 道樞 is the open space from which all perspectives can be reached.[33] Even if we cannot really *occupy* this place, we in effect gather it into our own perspective when we weaken our attachment to our own perspective and become open to others'.[34]

A maxim sometimes misattributed to Walt Whitman is: 'Be curious, not judgmental'. Our natural curiosity should lead us towards trying to see things from perspectives alien to our own, to understand what does not immediately make sense to us. Value judgements are always parochial. They divide a local context into good and bad, based on familiar qualities and recognizable patterns. But as you stray further from the context, the qualities become less familiar, the patterns are less recognizable, and your judgements miss the point. If you insist on holding fast to your values when the richness of the world escapes them, you have only two options. You can ignore alien contexts and insulate yourself in an intellectual province. Moral philosophers continue to appeal innocently to 'our intuitions', without thinking much about the cultural narrowness of the appeal.[35] Or you can take a distorted view that crops and squashes the world until it fits the compartments of your reductive value system. I once gave a public lecture that ranged across centuries and continents. Admittedly, it was excessively ambitious, and I expected to be pulled up on this. But, instead, the first question was from a man who told me he was having difficulty working out which side of British politics I was on.

The fullness of the world cannot be grasped from a single perspective. But we have the power to reach beyond our own viewpoint, to touch the pivot of the Dao and glimpse the world's true kaleidoscopic variety. What holds us back is our attachment to our value judgements, which keeps us solidly mired in our own provincial outlook. What explains this attachment, according to Zhuangzi, is our attachment to our identity.

Giving Up the Mutual Cultivation of Self and Things

Some evolutionary psychologists suggest that the original purpose for which humans developed their sense of self or identity was to participate in a moral community – to develop and maintain a reputation for upholding community-approved values and thus reap the benefits of cooperation within a group based on mutual trust.[36] Valuing and identity-forming are two sides of a single human activity, which we could call, borrowing an apt phrase from the title of Chinese philosopher Yang Guorong's recent book, 'the mutual cultivation of self and things'.[37] In carving up the world into good and bad, right and wrong, worthy and unworthy, successful and unsuccessful, *ran* 然 and *bu ran* 不然, *ke* 可 and *bu ke* 不可, you simultaneously build up a notion of your ideal, optimal self. In making value judgements, you define who you are, more than through any other human activity.[38]

A helpful example is given by the French-Lebanese author Amin Maalouf, who imagines asking a man in Sarajevo about his identity. In the 1980s the man might proudly declare himself to be a Yugoslavian. Twelve years later, during the Bosnian War, he might say that he is a Muslim, then add that he is a Bosnian. After the war, he might say *first* that he is a Bosnian, *then* that he is a Muslim: 'He'd tell you he was just on his way to the mosque, but he'd also want you to know that his country is part of Europe and that he hopes it will one day be a member of the Union.'[39] As the world changes, the man comes to value things differently, and as he values them differently he defines himself differently.

But if our sense of identity is tied up with the way that we value things, once we recognize that things do not absolutely have the values that they have from one limited perspective, we must recognize that our identity is likewise not absolute. Someone who is primarily a Bosnian from one point of view might be primarily a Muslim from another. From another again, these nuances might not appear at all. It depends what is important from that point of view. It is precisely this fluidity of identity that leads us to exert so much effort in curating and trying to control it. The experience of living in a foreign culture often involves a constant frustration of being defined by things you do not find important at all, while simultaneously having the things that do matter to you overlooked entirely, and immediately forgotten once pointed out.

The connection between identity and values also shows us why identity can be the site of intense conflict. An affront to your identity is a challenge to your values, and a challenge to your values threatens your very existence under your chosen definition. Worse still, since we are naturally inclined both to imitate and to seek to be imitated, our attachment to our own values in the face of a challenge provokes retaliation in the challenger. The harder each tries to make the other adopt her values, the harder each will resist. The positive feedback loop can escalate minor differences into full-scale ideological conflicts.

Things are not much better when values are shared, since rivalry can emerge over the status and prestige of each person's *exemplar*. Conflict arises over who is the moral paragon setting the example and who is the apprentice learning by imitating. Either way, in the unavoidable presence of other subjects, the entrenchment of value judgements and the assertion of identity feed on themselves and on each other.

Value Transformism

Zhuangzi's recommendation is to let go of both value judgements and identity.[40] It is easy to become enslaved to this practice, which intensifies in the face of external challenges and intensifies them in turn. If we can hold back from the value judgements, we can ease off on the identity-crafting. It helps to recognize the perspectival character of our value judgements. By doing so, they carry less weight. Everything that I say is good, right, *ran* 然, *ke* 可, from my perspective, is not from another's point of view. And there is no natural hierarchy or supremacy of perspectives – or at least any judgement ruling one perspective superior to another will itself be perspectival.

We do not need a collision with alien perspectives to realize the transformism of values. We can see how precarious and unstable our value judgements are from within our own perspective. An example is found in a story from the Han dynasty philosophical compilation, the *Huainanzi* 淮南子, which supposedly originated from a series of debates among various scholars, organized by the Prince of Huainan, Liu An (179–122 BCE). The story is:

> As for the revolutions and the mutual generation of calamity and good fortune, their alterations are difficult to perceive. At the near frontier, there was a [family of] skilled diviners whose horse suddenly became lost out among the Hu [people]. Everyone consoled them. The father said, 'This will quickly turn to good fortune!' After several months, the horse returned with a fine Hu steed. Everyone congratulated them. The father said, 'This will quickly turn to calamity!' The household was [now] replete with good horses; the son loved to ride, [but] he fell and broke his leg. Everyone consoled them. The father said, 'This will quickly turn to good fortune!' After one year, the Hu people entered the frontier in force; the able and strong all stretched their bowstrings and fought. Among the people of the near frontier, nine out of ten died. It was only because of lameness that father and son protected each other. Thus, / good fortune becoming calamity, / calamity becoming good fortune; / their transformations limitless, / so profound they cannot be fathomed.[41]

A similar sentiment is expressed by Yu Hua, when he reflects on how his highly disrupted education during the Cultural Revolution resulted in his learning only a limited stock of Chinese characters, which in turn resulted in the 'plain narrative language' for which he would later be praised as an author – sometimes compared to Ernest Hemingway. He reflects: 'Life is often this way: you may start off with an advantage, only to box yourself in over time, or sometimes you may start with a handicap, only to find it carries you a long way.' And then, with trademark winking irony, he quotes Mao: 'Good things can become bad, and bad things can become good.'[42] A sufficiently rich experience of life is enough to teach the transformism of values. Things are only ever good and bad *from here*, but *here* is a shifting and unstable place. Chapter 5 of the *Zhuangzi*, *Dechong fu* 德充符 ('Tally of Virtue Replete'), teaches this lesson through the example of figures with various deformities and disabilities, who find, through a shift in perspective, that their 'handicaps' are actually advantages.[43]

To insist that the world *absolutely is* the way your judgements rule it to be is to attempt to enforce an Aristotelian law of identity upon a nature that has no respect for it. It is a domineering and egotistical practice. It is also untruthful. The indigenous Australian philosopher Tyson Yunkaporta draws a similar lesson from a traditional story about the 'moon sisters', who tried to spear the moon reflected on the surface of the sea at night, believing it to be a luminous fish. Because the reflection shifted along with their perspective, they were unable to catch it. 'Now you can see their shadows in the moon where they remain trapped to this day, a warning to all about chasing the illusion of fixed viewpoints.'[44] If you do not want to end up like the moon sisters, Yunkaporta warns: 'You must allow yourself to be transformed through your interactions with other agents and the knowledge that passes through you from them.'[45] This means being flexible on the value judgements that, in addition to defining our identity, often appear to give our world its meaning.

A stark contrast to Yunkaporta's attitude can be found in the contemporary American philosopher Susan Wolf. She argues that finding true, absolute meaning in the world involves acknowledging that 'some things are better than others [. . .] people, for example, are better than rocks or mosquitoes, and a Vermeer painting is better than the scraps on my compost heap'.[46] But Yunkaporta tells us: 'Anyone who thinks they're better than a rock should be turned into one – then they would find out they're not that special, and they could finally be happy.'[47] What he calls on us to recognize here involves giving up on a meaningful world in Wolf's sense. But, if Yunkaporta and Zhuangzi are right, the compensating gain is the chance of real happiness and avoiding the fate of the moon sisters.

In the anti-essentialist, transformist vision of the world presented in the *Zhuangzi*, things are always *not* what we deem them to be, especially on matters of value, no matter how insistently we deem them to be so. They are as we deem them from one perspective, but they are equally not so from another, and perspectives themselves are far from stable – shifting like the moon's reflection and never to be caught. Likewise, as we have seen, our real self – our *wu* 吾 – will never be successfully defined by any of the identities – *wo* 我 – that we try to impose on it. The mutual cultivation of self and things is an attempt to impose a value-laden identity on a self and a world that fundamentally resist the imposition. It is a fight against, not the essence of the universe, but its fundamental *inessentiality*: its transformism. Nobody can win this fight; you can only end up enslaved to it. We would be happier and more peaceful letting things flow, vanish, transform, be indistinct, be ambiguous – letting our perspective touch the pivot of the Dao. Rather than trying to be ourselves, we are better off vanishing and transforming into others. Identity is not the way. It is not the way of things, and it is not the way for us.

PART TWO
Spinoza

4.
Persevering in Your Being

Death of a Social Organism

The cultural memory of the Warring States period is funerary, elegiac. Something vast and total – the Zhou dynasty, along with its governing order (*zheng* 政) and its ways of living (*dao* 道) – has been lost. There is poetry mourning its end, and eccentric attempts by Confucians to revive it over the centuries.

Contrast this with the cultural memory of the world of Benedict de Spinoza (1632–77), born Baruch Spinoza in the Dutch Republic of the early modern period. The record of this period is not funereal; it is nativity. The beginnings of modern science, capitalism, the secular state and liberalism are all traced to this point in space and time. It is the era in which great colonial empires were launched, whose imprint and legacy are still so much with us. Today these conjure memories of brutality and destruction, but to Europeans at the time they heralded new beginnings in new worlds.[1]

Living in Amsterdam in 1631, the great French philosopher René Descartes (1596–1650) – commonly regarded as the father of modern philosophy – wrote to a friend back in France:

> Whenever you have the pleasure of seeing the fruit growing in your orchards and of feasting your eyes on its abundance, bear in mind that it gives me just as much pleasure to watch

> the ships arriving, laden with all the produce of the Indies and all the rarities of Europe. Where else on earth could you find, as easily as you do here, all the conveniences of life and all the curiosities you could hope to see?[2]

Marvelling at the social achievements of the new republic, he went on: 'In what other country could you find such complete freedom, or sleep with less anxiety, or find armies at the ready to protect you, or find fewer poisonings, or acts of treason or slander?'[3] The capital of the Dutch Republic struck its philosophical guest as modern, efficient and comfortable.

But the death of something was also felt during this period. During the centuries before the early modern period, society had been regarded as an *organism* like the human body. The historian of early capitalism R. H. Tawney describes how the new commercial societies of Western Europe emerged from this earlier organic conception, in which society was 'composed of different members', each with its own unique role and purpose: 'prayer, or defence, or merchandise, or tilling the soil'. In this pre-modern social conception, there had to be inequality among classes, since each class defined the role that its members were to play and the shares that they were permitted to claim.[4] A monk prayed, and was given the subsistence to do so, because he was a monk. A soldier defended the nation and claimed the soldier's share. A peasant tilled the soil on account of her peasantry and rendered to her feudal superior the portion due to him as such. This is a picture of another governing sociopolitical order – a *zheng* 政. William Shakespeare, writing in the waning days of this pre-modern social order, uses the word 'degree' as a near equivalent to *zheng* 政. His Ulysses (a character from the ancient world but obviously speaking to Shakespeare's contemporaries) sternly reminds us that:

The heavens themselves, the planets and this centre
Observe degree, priority and place,
Insisture, course, proportion, season, form,
Office and custom, in all line of order.

– *Troilus and Cressida* (I.iii.89–92)

The natural order of Shakespeare's time, dying though it was, had priorities and places for peasants, lords, craftsmen and merchants as well as planets. How they were to act was determined by what they were – their superlunary essence in the case of the planets, their born station and its duties in the case of people.

Tawney is clear that pre-modern reality often diverged from this ideal. But the death of this ideal is what he chronicles. The image of the social organism was slowly being replaced by an image of individuals striving to get what they can – sometimes cooperating, sometimes conflicting, but in any case seeking to better *themselves*. One illustration of this shift is the transformation of the notion of the law of nature. Medieval writers wrote of the law of nature as 'a moral restraint upon economic self-interest'. But in the modern period – the sixteenth and seventeenth centuries in Western Europe – a notion of natural right emerged to replace this law of nature. This modern idea of natural right connoted 'not divine ordinance, but human appetites'. 'Natural rights were invoked by the individualism of the age as a reason why self-interest should be given free play.'[5]

Spinoza, born in 1632 into the Amsterdam whose modernity so impressed Descartes, was part of this change. He asserts in one of his political writings that the *right of nature* is 'nothing but the rules of the nature of each individual, according to which we conceive each to be determined to a certain way of existing and acting'.[6] He rejects the idea of a law of nature, which restrains individuals, in favour of a conception in which the *right* of nature is simply the combined rights of individuals to act as far as their power permits. And, citing a proverb famously illustrated in a 1557 engraving by Pieter Bruegel the Elder – *Big Fish Eat Little Fish* – he adds that when the big fish do so it is 'by the highest right of nature'. As for human beings, their natural right is 'not determined by sound reason but by desire and power'.[7]

What was vanishing was, in Tawney's words, 'the conception of a rule of life superior to individual desires and temporary exigencies, which was what the medieval theorist meant by "natural law"'.[8] Replacing it was a conception of the right of nature as the aggregate outcome of individual desires, each expressed to the limit of its power. The final draft of this conception would be the notion of a *market outcome*: the always-partly-mythical basis of social organization in a capitalist society, said (in the guiding myth) to bubble up spontaneously from the free exercise of individual preferences.

Spinoza's society had not quite reached that stage. There are competing theories about why the Dutch Republic did not become fully capitalist in the way that industrial Britain would.[9] One important point is that rank and station – official position in the social organism – still determined economic outcomes to a significant extent.[10] Still, the thought had emerged that the social system at its core is not an organism governed by a natural law superior to individual desires but rather a combinatory result of power struggles among those individual desires themselves.

This new vision of society does not deny the existence of the old natural law. Rather, it explains that it also is the product of desire and power. Powerful agents, desiring that others live in a certain way, use their power to impose that way of living as a 'natural' law, through both coercion and psychological manipulation. Legislators impose such a law, writes Spinoza, 'to restrain the crowd, as if bridling a horse'.[11]

Confession and Identity

At least as important in understanding Spinoza's context is the new form of religion that emerged in this period. The seismic event that preceded him was what we can broadly call the Protestant Reformation.[12] It was a sort of fission reaction. In 1517, Martin Luther (1483–1546), an Augustinian friar and theologian, broke from the Catholic church, followed by others who then broke from him, and then from each other, and so on. Attempting to come to terms with this, the original Catholic church underwent divisions of its own.

By Spinoza's age, however, something else had begun to happen. The different religious groups into which the Reformation had divided believers began to define themselves with increasing narrowness and precision – a process known to historians as 'confessionalization'.[13] While dividing against each other, the new and old religious sects or 'confessions' were freshly defining themselves and seeking to maintain internal cohesion. The fission reaction was controlled.

The end-product of this was a new sort of religious identity, based on confessional loyalties rather than social rank and station.[14] A Protestant merchant had a basis for new feelings of superiority towards a Catholic lord, altogether different from the old order of social rank. The demand for this new form of identity drove individuals to confrontation and exclusion and to put pressure on others to form identities. Thus, the era was full of evangelical zeal and eagerness to make confessional identities fully transparent, for example through tell-tale conventions of dress and hairstyle. The new kind of identity invaded the social organism, introducing new divisions among those who had previously belonged together and creating new status hierarchies orthogonal to those that had existed before.

Both the economic and religious changes connected to an emerging fear that was spreading across Western European society, which is the subject of the American literary critic Lionel Trilling's classic study of changing notions of selfhood in the modern era, *Sincerity and Authenticity*. The sixteenth century, Trilling tells us, 'was preoccupied to an extreme degree with dissimulation, feigning, and pretence'.[15] The picaresque novels of this time, some of which Spinoza had in his library, are full of comedic situations arising from imposture, fakery, and occasionally delusion regarding social position. The spectre of capitalist self-interest – of individuals all getting what they can by graft or guile – raises the threat of insincerity further. People often stand to gain by pretending to be what they are not. If individual desire and power are the only right of nature, nobody can be sure that a professed merchant is really a merchant, an apparent peasant really a peasant, someone dressed as a noblewoman really a noblewoman. Playing these roles are self-serving individuals, who are only as sincere as it benefits them to be.

Even more profound is the fear of confessional insincerity: people insincerely pretending to hold religious beliefs in order to fit in. To guard against this constant catechizing, tests of faith and secret shibboleths emerged during this period. Spinoza himself was born into a community whose confessional identity was troubled – the Amsterdam Jewish community composed largely of refugees from the Inquisition in Spain and its equivalent in Portugal. Many of them had, under duress, converted to Christianity, hence they were commonly called *conversos*, yet they privately retained their Jewish beliefs and practices. Not only had the members of this community been forced into fakery, their attempts to recover their own *true* religious identity, once they found relative sanctuary in a more tolerant Amsterdam, were obstructed by a loss of cultural memory. Their oppressors had stamped out many of the traces of the old rites and beliefs that defined this identity and they were left trying to reconstruct these as best they could.[16] They were insincerely Christian while struggling to be authentically Jewish.

An Age of Authenticity

Of this age, then, Confucius and Shakespeare's Ulysses would lament. It was an age in which merchants might not be merchants, lords not lords, *conversos* not *conversos* – an epoch without 'degree' or *zheng* 政. But Trilling observes how the idea of sincerity, and the paranoia around it, drove the early modern period towards another idea: *authenticity*.[17] In the ideal social organism, roles are exhaustively definitive. To meet a priest or a soldier is primarily to meet the *role* and only secondarily to meet the person playing it. But as the social organism begins to die, we enter a world in which the real person lurks in the shadows. Once opened, this chasm between reality and presentation can never be closed. A soldier might be perfectly sincere in his soldiering. Still, the very fact that he *is* sincere reveals that he *might not* have been, and might, in certain circumstances, *stop being*. The man is only contingently a soldier.

Soldiering defines the role but not the man who plays it. So what defines the man? This is the question of authenticity.

Authenticity stands for an identity that runs deeper than sincere commitment to an assigned social station. It stands for an identity that is fixed by nature, not by individual commitment or social assignment. Bootle, whose essays on identity we have quoted above, explains authenticity as follows: 'The foundational idea of authenticity is that a unique, true self exists within each of us – a "real me" that is separate from all the things that are not the real me.'[18] We need to navigate our lives around each other, and for this we must have some sense of who or what we are navigating around. Once sincerity is in question, social role is not enough. We want to know the *true nature* of the creatures we are dealing with. And once we are thinking like this, we will, naturally enough, want to know *our own* true nature.

We have already seen Spinoza speaking of the 'rules of the nature of each individual' in the passage quoted above, which is taken from his *Theological-Political Treatise* (1670) – a book Spinoza interrupted his philosophical work to write, in order to defend the 'freedom to philosophize' against religious and political oppression. Passages like this suggest that he is a philosopher of authenticity. I do not blame other scholars for thinking so. But the passages are misleading. A very different message is found in his major philosophical work, *Ethics Demonstrated in Geometrical Order*, which he worked on for several years and was published after his death in 1677. Spinoza claims here that we each have a nature, determining our way of existing and acting. But reading *Ethics* more closely, we see that he does not claim that we are born with this nature, nor that we discover it by looking within. Rather, like Zhuangzi, he suggests that we acquire it by copying from models. And, also like Zhuangzi, he believes that in our highest state – the state of beatitude – we can stop doing this.

Spinoza was, we can safely assume, led to this conclusion not only by his philosophy but also by his life.[19] At the age of twenty-three, he was expelled from the Jewish community of Amsterdam, most likely on account of heretical opinions he refused to recant. Entirely cut off from his family and the life he had known, Spinoza had to find a new place for himself: learning Latin, changing his name from the Hebrew 'Baruch' to the Latin 'Benedict', and mastering the craft of lens grinding to earn a living. Banned from the synagogue, he never officially converted to Christianity, although he befriended Christians of various sects, especially radical Protestants.[20] In an age where identity was defined by confessional affiliation, Spinoza was unique in belonging to no church whatsoever. Removed from his native community, he remained a foreigner in the Dutch Republic, excusing himself in one letter for the inadequacy of his Dutch.[21] Nor was his class identity clear. Born to a merchant family, he had become a manual worker, yet his intellectual achievements brought him into contact with the greatest scientists and politicians of his age. Like Zhuangzi, his reputation brought an offer of high station – in his case, a professorship at Heidelberg University. And, again like Zhuangzi, he rejected it, preferring a life of humble freedom. His contemporaries must have been at a loss to know quite what to make of him or how to identify him. And in *Ethics*, his great philosophical masterpiece, he would present the lesson that true salvation can only come from escaping identity: 'To disinhabit ourselves, and thereby save ourselves,' as Rebecca Goldstein puts it in her biographical study of Spinoza.[22] To present this picture of salvation,

Spinoza developed the most advanced psychological theory of his age.

Although Spinoza is most recognized for his abstract, quasi-mathematical reasoning, *Ethics* is full of insights that could only have come from close observation of human conduct. Spinoza's project is to prove the psychological theory he drew from life on the basis of 'geometrical' reasoning: deduction from fundamental axioms. *Ethics* thus takes the reader on a journey, beginning with abstract reasoning about the general nature of reality, through a theory of the human mind, to an analysis of the mechanisms governing human emotion, and finally ending with a vision of salvation.

Desire as Self-Preservation

The psychological theory of *Ethics* begins with a proposition that applies far beyond the human case: 'each thing, insofar as it can, strives to persevere in its being' (E 3p6).[23] This at first seems like the sort of grand metaphysical platitude that is too general to be meaningful, lumping together diverse phenomena according to vague patterns. The planet Venus 'strives to persevere in its being' insofar as gravitational fields preserve its spheroid shape and orbit around the Sun. Moreover, like every other body, it will return to thermic equilibrium following disruption. This is quite different from saying that a lizard 'strives to persevere in its being', meaning that it will, for example, search for water when it is thirsty. The causes are completely different, and they do not seem the sort of thing to be proven by general metaphysical reasoning.

On the other hand, perhaps there is a level of scientific generality at which Spinoza's claim can be asserted as something close to a metaphysical truth, or at least a fundamental statistical law. In a complex world, in which diverse and opposing forces are always at play, the presence of an enduring structure or pattern signals a very high probability that some stable equilibrium has been reached among these forces. Forces that would otherwise destroy or transform the thing are very likely balanced against countervailing forces. We can call the maintenance of this equilibrium the thing's 'striving', whether it is a balance of gravitational and electrostatic forces maintaining a body's shape, energy transfers underpinning thermic equilibrium or a balance of evolutionary adaptations against an environment hostile to an organism's life.

Human beings, however, are conscious. We are *aware* of threats to our existence and of our striving to resist them. Spinoza understands *desire* as consciousness of this striving (E 3p9s).[24] What I experience as my desire is in fact my consciousness of some self-perpetuating tendency – some set of survival mechanisms. Desire is consciousness of my struggle to continue in being. All other desires are instrumental towards the ultimate end of continuing to exist.

Desire is not the same as appetite. Spinoza describes desire as appetite along with consciousness. This is puzzling, since appetites are already conscious, and Spinoza admits this.[25] There must then be a difference between an appetite *being conscious* and its being what Spinoza calls *accompanied by consciousness*. Spinoza must think of the consciousness involved in desire as a type of *self*-consciousness. If I have an *appetite* such as hunger, I am conscious of the urge for food – indeed preoccupied with thoughts of food. But if I have a *desire* for a smart suit of clothes, I think about *myself* wearing the suit, swanning into parties and turning heads. Desiring a house is desiring to *be the sort of person* who lives in or owns that house.

Desiring a romantic partner is desiring to *be* that person's romantic partner.

This does not mean that desire is essentially selfish. In true romantic love, for example, you might see selfless devotion to a partner as essential to your true being. But it does mean that all desire is *egotistical*. All desire is centred fundamentally upon a conception of self that it aims to realize.

The above examples of egotistical desire are the more palatable ones. Others are far more embarrassing and harder to admit. In Evelyn Waugh's *Decline and Fall*, the prison governor, Sir Wilfred Lucas-Dockerty, is driven by a desire to improve the lives of prisoners and society as a whole. But running secretly in his mind are excerpts from an imaginary history of a great prison reformer – himself.[26] We desire great moral triumphs in the world. But, when we wrench these desires out of their framing and see them plainly, we are sometimes embarrassed to discover their hidden egotism – to find that they are really desires *to be* the hero fighting for the great causes. The slogan, 'Be the change you want to see in the world', conveys a double-edged truth. As one moral philosopher puts it: 'A view of what you ought to do is a view of who you are.'[27] Morality bottoms out in identity.

Persevere in Being What?

Spinoza writes that 'desire is the very essence of a human being' (E 3app1).[28] To continue to be, in a world full of dangers and opposing forces, you must *strive* to be. But to be what? Spinoza writes that each thing strives to continue in *its being*: '*suo esse*'. In medieval philosophy, '*esse*' typically refers to being of some certain definite form. For example, Thomas Aquinas

(1225/7–1274), the leading philosophical authority of the late medieval period, holds that 'every *esse* exists according to some form'.[29] To be conscious of yourself as striving to continue in your being, you must have a notion of what your being is. If I point at a caterpillar transforming within its cocoon, and ask if it is persevering in its being, you cannot begin to answer without deciding what its being consists of. It is ceasing to be a caterpillar but flourishing as a metamorphic organism. Likewise, when you observe yourself undergoing a change, it can be either deterioration or development, depending on the description under which you identify yourself.

Conscious striving to persevere in your being thus requires a conscious notion of your self – your authentic identity. The great twentieth-century French Spinozist Alexandre Matheron argues that we can view Spinoza's 'striving' as a kind of life-drive in which 'to live is to live *according to my individual essence*'. All desires are thus 'reduced to fragmentary aspects and partial consequences of a more fundamental desire, which is simply for a self'.[30] But, as the saying goes, I cannot be what I cannot see. Desire requires some picture, however vague, of the identity I am trying to realize in the world. Where do I find such a picture?

As we have seen already, it is impossible to simply *observe* your authentic self, since the authentic self is always yet to be realized. You can observe any number of things about yourself, but nothing tells you that these define you. Some might be alien distortions of your authentic identity. Some might be part of the chrysalis you need to shed for your true self to emerge. Others might be unchangeable but still accidental blemishes upon your true identity, rather than expressions of it.

Some people try to simply stipulate what makes for true identity. *The Impact of Identity: The Power of Knowing Who You*

Are, by Irina Nevzlin, an Israeli entrepreneur, begins with a moving description of how she rediscovered her Jewish roots, which her family, living in Soviet Russia, had suppressed. Even after she learned that she was Jewish, 'nobody would talk to me about it'.[31] During the collapse of Soviet Communism, Nevzlin found that by identifying with her family history and learning more about it she achieved a sense of stable meaning, built upon an identity that is *given* and not *chosen*: 'Being part of a people is not a superficial identity. Nor is it a label you apply, like liberal, musician, vegan, or businessman. It's something essential you are born into and a deep part of you that will never change.'[32]

Yet Nevzlin admits: 'You might like your roots, and feel connected to them, or decide to ignore them.'[33] Even if you ignore your ancestry, she points out, 'It's part of who you are.'[34] That, of course, begs the question. Some will say that being a liberal, musician, vegan or businessperson is far more expressive of their true identity – their deep, authentic self – than the mere accident of their family history. There is no law of nature ruling that only inborn and unchanging traits can define *who you truly are*. We can only speculate about the complex feelings with which Spinoza must have considered his own roots in a community that had rejected him.[35]

Desire as Mimetic

Desire in Spinoza's theory must be built around a model of an authentic self. This model cannot be directly deduced from self-observation. It reflects an aspiration, not an established fact. Whence do we derive the image of the self we aspire to have, the authentic identity we strive to realize?

Spinoza's answer is that we derive our sense of self in the first instance by imitation. This theory is not explicit in the text of *Ethics*. But after many years of studying it, I am convinced that this idea represents the best way to make sense of various claims made in the book.[36] Spinoza gives star billing in Part Three of *Ethics*, 'Of the Nature and Origin of Emotions', to what he calls *emulation*: 'the desire for a thing which is generated in us from the fact that we imagine others like us to have the same desire' (E 3p27s).[37] Why should what *others* desire determine what *we* desire? Because these others *model being* to us. We have seen that mere introspection does not tell us what our fundamental, true being is. We cannot see our own true self directly. Where else can we look for it but to others? As Aristotle writes: 'when we wish to see our own face, we do so by looking into the mirror; in the same way, when we wish to know ourselves, we can obtain that knowledge by looking at our friend' (1213a20–26).[38] Our friends, our neighbours or our peers give us our first clue as to what our authentic self might be.

But this is not all. Modelling our desires on others, we develop what Spinoza calls *ambition*: a person's urge 'that everyone should love what he loves and hate what he hates' (E 3p31c).[39] As discussed in Chapter 2, this is to be expected, given that our models are, by definition, *exemplary*. If we want to be like them, we want to be exemplary too. It is mysterious why people become so hostile, angry and sometimes cruel towards those who listen to the 'wrong' sort of music, wear the 'wrong' sort of clothing, support the 'wrong' politics (where doing so is unlikely to make any difference to electoral outcomes), cheer for the 'wrong' teams, etc. But some of it might be explained by the implicit affront to their *ambition*. There you are, modelling the correct preferences, and these despicable ingrates reject the guidance you have so generously offered! Spinoza lived in a world where people were executed for preferring the wrong interpretations of Scripture, so perhaps he had a clearer view of a social pathology that now works through more insidious and psychologically sophisticated channels.

The effect of this dynamic of ambition is to generate what Spinoza calls *glory*: 'joy taken in some action of ours, which we imagine others to praise' (E 4def.aff.30).[40] Indeed, Spinoza's alternative definition of ambition is 'immoderate desire for glory' (E 4def.aff.44). Since what we ultimately seek is *to be our true self*, our highest good (E 4p52) is what Spinoza calls 'self-acquiescence' (*acquiescentia in se ipso*), which means the feeling of having arrived at such being. Since we model this being on exemplars, we want to be exemplary ourselves. We want from others admiration, praise and above all *imitation* (the highest form of flattery). This comes in the form of what Spinoza calls *vainglory*, or empty glory:

> What is called empty glory [*gloria vana*] is self-acquiescence that is supported only by public opinion. When that ceases, acquiescence itself (that is, the highest good that each one loves) ceases. Whence it happens that whoever glories in the opinion of the crowd struggles every day – acts and strives in anxious concern to preserve a reputation. For the crowd is various and inconstant, and thus a reputation, unless protected, soon fades away.
>
> Indeed, because everyone desires to capture the applause of the crowd, one person readily puts down the reputation of another. From this, seeing that the good contended for is judged to be supreme, an enormous lust arises to dominate the other in any possible way. And whoever turns out the victor glories more in having harmed the other than in having

> profited himself. And therefore this glory or acquiescence is really empty, for it is nothing. (E 4p58s)

This, then, is the straight line Spinoza traces from identity to vainglory. It is his version of the religious story of the Fall of humanity.

5.
The Fall

Crowd-Sourcing Identity

It is hardly news that humans seek high status and glory. More unusual is the theory that they do so simply as a consequence of trying to be themselves. To understand this idea, it is worth considering why we develop an identity at all.

In the previous chapter we noted how the question of the *authentic self* becomes especially salient during the collapse of a sincerity regime. When social roles are no longer expected to fully determine behaviour, the question of deeper character must arise. We have seen that, although some will resent the analogy, Spinoza is like modern evolutionary psychologists in one way. He seeks to explain features of human psychology in terms of a struggle for survival: the striving of each thing to persevere in its being. And evolutionary psychologists have for some time explained the emergence of identity in terms of the survival value of a good reputation, which attracts the protection and good favour of a social group.[1]

The contemporary primatologist Richard Wrangham tells a hypothetical story, according to which humans overcame their tendency to what he calls 'reactive aggression' – the sort of violence you might encounter in a tough schoolyard or on a mean street – through a process of self-domestication.[2] Compared with other primates, we show a low tendency towards reactive aggression. But we score off the charts for 'proactive aggression' – premeditated, organized and institutionalized violence. Wrangham's self-domestication story aims to explain this skew. But his story also sheds light on the connection between identity and glory.

According to Wrangham, domestication occurs over a long period of time, during which the more aggressive members of a species are eliminated or prevented from reproducing. Humans, he shows, display several physical signs of being domesticated, known as the 'domestication syndrome'. But who domesticated us? Although early thinkers on the topic proposed that we were domesticated by God, a naturalistic answer is that we domesticated ourselves. Over generations, humans weeded aggressive individuals from their own gene pool. Wrangham calls this dark story the *execution hypothesis*: 'The execution hypothesis [. . .] proposes that selection against aggressiveness and in favour of greater docility came from execution of the most antisocial individuals.'[3]

But many aggressive and antisocial individuals are dangerous – strong and violent. Who was brave enough to eliminate them? Coalitions. A coalition has strength in numbers, but only insofar as bonds of trust and loyalty hold it together. Various proposals have been made as to why humans developed a special ability to form coalitions. Some identify opposable thumbs and the ability to use projectiles as the crucial feature, suggesting that the ability to attack from a distance reduced the risk to each member of the coalition in the event that their peers fled the field of battle.[4] Wrangham rejects this, believing rather that language played a crucial role.[5] Whatever the cause, the human capacity for coalition-forming allows proactive aggression to drive out reactive aggression. Premeditated, pragmatic violence on the part of groups controls instinctive, emotional violence on the part of individuals.

The premeditated nature of proactive aggression makes it terrifying but predictable. These are two things that reactive aggression is not. Of course, reactive aggression is scary, often *because* it is unpredictable. But proactive aggression is beyond frightening. You can stand down a bully, but not a coalition bent on meting out justice. Defiance will only fuel their righteous rage. On the other hand, there is a practicable system for avoiding proactive aggression: play by the social rules.

Now a complex game develops. When proactive, coalitional violence is well established, antisocial individuals know to hide their antisociality. The imperative of the coalition is therefore to look, not for overt signs of antisociality, but rather for *anything out of the ordinary*, as the anti-terrorism announcements on public transport say. Any sign of stepping outside the ordinary rules of conduct, any nonconformity with the dominant culture's norms and values, can be enough to alert a coalition scanning for internal enemies hiding in the community. So the rule for avoiding proactive violence becomes: *conform*.

Borrowing a term from the twentieth-century sociologist Ernest Gellner, Wrangham describes this situation as the 'tyranny of the cousins': 'Cousins', in the context of a small-scale society, is a metaphor for the group of adults whose decisions hold sway. Their power is absolute. If you do not conform to their dictates, you are in danger.[6] The cousins monitor potential threats to the community by ascribing to each of us a sort of moral identity – an inner character – as a predictive model of our potentially antisocial behaviour, just as the emperors of the Northern and Southern Seas drilled a face onto Hundun.[7]

If the cousins draw the wrong face upon you, the results can be deadly.

We do not always live under the tyranny of the cousins now, although it seems to re-emerge very naturally under the right conditions.[8] But if something like the above evolutionary story is true, the same process that eliminated antisocial individuals from our population is likely to have selected for extreme vigilance concerning moral reputation – or, more generally, identity-consciousness. Human self-domestication attached survival value to caring about who you are in the eyes of others. Our ancestors *had* to care, to secure the protection of the cousins rather than their wrath.

Crowds and the State

Alexandre Matheron, the twentieth-century French Spinozist we met in the previous chapter, finds a version of the execution hypothesis in Spinoza.[9] Spinoza had originally explained the origins of the state in terms of a traditional 'social contract' – a rational decision by individuals to combine into a political order.[10] But in his mysterious *Political Treatise*, a book which was not completed before he died, Spinoza argues that 'we must seek the causes and natural foundation of the state not from the teachings of reason but rather from the common nature or condition of human beings'.[11] Experience perhaps had suggested to him that human reason is too feeble a foundation for human cooperation.[12]

Something odd occurs when Spinoza comes to explain this affective foundation of political order – an intersection between his psychological and political theory that Matheron's close studies were some of the first to elucidate. Spinoza observes that 'humans are led more by affect than reason'. Therefore 'a crowd is naturally led to agree, not by reason but by some shared affect'. Its members have 'a shared hope, or fear, or a desire to avenge some shared harm'.[13] Here Spinoza refers back to an earlier passage. Matheron notices that this referenced passage 'is devoted, not at all to the causes of the *existence* of the State, but on the contrary to the causes of its *dissolution*'.[14]

The referenced passage states that since 'humans are led by nature to conspire in one act either out of a shared hope, or fear, or a desire to avenge some shared harm', the power of the state is *weakened* 'to the extent that it gives causes for many to conspire in one act', presumably of rebellion.[15] Spinoza appears to be saying that indignation *creates* the State in the same way it can destroy it.[16]

To understand this, we must turn to Spinoza's theory of imitation. A crucial statement in *Ethics* is: 'the very property of human nature, from which it follows that human beings are compassionate, also leads them to be envious and ambitious' (E 3p32s).[17] Our compassion stems from our emulative striving to feel what others feel. But from the same striving we develop ambition – the craving to influence others. And when we influence them, we create potential rivals. If I make you desire what I desire, and you end up with more of it than I have, then I thereby equip myself with a ready source of envy. For this reason, human conflict emerges very naturally from human nature. But then emulation drives a new social tendency. As Matheron puts it: 'all aggression has witnesses which, by affective imitation, become indignant against those who they consider to be the aggressor and come to the aid of those who they consider to be the victim.'[18] A crowd emerges around one party to the conflict, emulating her hostility towards the other party.

Which side the crowd takes depends on minor initial differences, which become exponentially amplified through the mimetic dynamics of the system. If, for instance, two bystanders take my side and only one takes yours, an ambitious bystander desiring the approval of the maximum number will be slightly inclined to side with me. The next bystander will face a stronger motivation to join my side, and so on until a crowd has formed around me, and the tyranny of the cousins is clearly on my side. Your supporters then face a strong incentive to defect.

The first result of this is the emergence of 'the power of all', which is strikingly similar to Gellner's tyranny of the cousins. Since this power is driven by emulation, it will naturally align itself with whichever of the adversaries most resembles the crowd: 'the one who has more or less the same desires and the same values and who possesses more or less the same things'. From this emerges a human community, governed by social norms, and then, eventually, a political system.[19] Spinoza thus finds the origins of the State in the tyranny of the cousins. The pivotal moment is when the dynamics of emulation create a punitive crowd, enforcing moral and cultural norms as the traits it deems as marking appropriate resemblance to the crowd.

These norms also define the range of acceptable identities: the types of things that you must be in order to be on the side of the crowd. Identities are thus born out of violence, specifically political violence, which defines political identities through inclusion and exclusion.[20] The initial pressure towards identity is pressure to identify with political violence.

From this the whole range of social roles, hierarchies and institutions that define the political order can emerge. Spinoza views the origins of the State as 'democratic' in a certain sense (the *demos* in question being not the whole people but the cousins, the crowd). But the origin of its force is the spontaneous formation of punitive coalitions.[21] Spinoza's theory of the violent origins of political institutions is an early version of the execution hypothesis.

Conformity and Glory

The members of a crowd are also driven by an imperative to demonstrate their commitment to the crowd's norms. So strongly do they identify with those norms that they are ready to condemn and discipline transgressors – at least, it benefits them to *appear* ready to do so. Instances of this were observed in the Second World War: people were driven to commit barbarous acts out of fear, not of direct punishment but of 'a dramatic lowering of their esteem within the group'.[22] Fear of lowered esteem is in fact the primary lever by which the power of the crowd moves individuals. Although subtle, it is much more powerful than the fear of overt punishment.

Spinoza is aware of this point.[23] The key to the full explanation of the crowd's power over us is our own desire for glory, which is simply the flip side of the fear of collective disapproval. Spinoza defines *shame* as 'sadness concomitant with the idea of some action of ours, which we imagine others to disparage' (E 3def.aff.31), while glory is 'joy concomitant with the idea of some actions of ours, which we imagine others to praise' (E 3def.aff.30).[24] These affects are essentially imitations of the crowd's disapproval or approval. We internalize its judgemental feelings towards us.

Glory and reputation in the eyes of the crowd are crucial for the development of political institutions.[25] Spinoza proposes that what keeps people from breaking the social contract is their fear of appearing foolish (*ne mente carere videatur*).[26] The scholar Eva Debray explains how 'the fear of passing for a fool is, at its root, the fear of attracting the reproving, contemptuous gaze of the group'.[27] Spinoza's social-contract theory is very different from a theory based on rational individual decisions, which is found throughout the liberal tradition. In Spinoza's version, people fear breaking the social contract for the same reason that they fear turning up to a gala event in unfashionable shoes or finding themselves in a conversation where everyone but them seems to have mastered the appropriate slang or academic jargon. Such *faux pas* signal unawareness of the sophisticated norms of a group, and thus a blundering violation of the social contract. It is not simply *dangerous* to flout norms when the cousins are on watch. Worse than that, it is *embarrassing*.

Shame, after all, can be at least as hard to endure as physical pain. Wrangham tells of an experiment in which subjects are at first included in a game with strangers and then, after a few minutes, excluded without explanation. The subjects demonstrate 'sadness, anger, and a series of negative effects including feelings of alienation, depression, helplessness, and even a reduced sense of meaning in life', as well as 'elevated activation of a part of the brain, the dorsal anterior cingulate cortex, that is also activated by physical pain'.[28] The pain experienced here is attached to a loss of status, which is identity in the eyes of others.

Again, we have a self-perpetuating mechanism. The power of the crowd drives you to care about your identity, and the more you care, the more the crowd has power over you. Having the crowd change its mind about you provokes feelings of panic. We can see in a new light Spinoza's statement that 'whoever glories in the opinion of the crowd struggles every day – acts and strives in anxious concern to preserve a reputation' (E 4p58). The crowd demands identity from us, but we can never be secure in the identity we form in the shadow of its power, since 'the crowd is various and inconstant, and thus a reputation, unless protected, soon fades away'. In his *Theologico-Political Treatise*, Spinoza comments on the crowd's tendency 'now to adore their kings as very gods and then to execrate and detest them as the common plague of all humanity'.[29] What goes for kings goes for anyone who achieves glory. If you win over the crowd, you become a model for those seeking to do the same. Now you have envious rivals, looking for the smallest mistake or slightest blemish to provide an opportunity to dethrone you.

The Fall to Identity

All things strive to persevere in being, according to Spinoza, but humans strive for it *consciously*. This means striving to be *something in particular*, to have *some particular identity*. Underpinning this striving is the power of the crowd, who are searching for your authentic self as a reliable predictive model of your action. You had better have the right sort of identity to stay on the right side. But the culture of *authenticity*, which emerges in the collapse of a sincerity regime, gives this a paradoxical twist. You cannot appear to be cultivating your identity *only* to appease the crowd, since in that case your identity is thoroughly inauthentic – a cunning mask. Trying to *appear* conformist is just what a crafty antisocial transgressor would do.

Therefore, you must rather appear to *just happen* to be what the crowd wants you to be, naturally and spontaneously. Your *aspirational* being must be defined in terms of an exemplar, while your *occurrent* being – what you happen to be – is a mere unstable chaos from which different strands can always be pulled out and emphasized. To quote Bootle again: 'Authenticity demands that we *don't* conform to expectations: that we are purely, exquisitely ourselves; that our inner self overcomes any constraints the outer world may impose.'[30] Bootle is well aware that the word 'demands' drives a paradox right through this sentence. The *demand* of authenticity is one of the constraints that the outer world imposes, so the demand to be 'purely, exquisitely ourselves', in defiance of those constraints, is logically impossible to satisfy.

All the same, as Spinoza acknowledges, the drive to satisfy this need is the very foundation of human sociability.[31] It is the transmission belt of human culture. The economist Joan Robinson once wrote: 'Ambition and the love of praise is how a child learns to walk.'[32] We become ourselves by aiming to impress others, and this requires pretending that we are not trying to impress them at all. This diabolical conspiracy between authenticity and conformity allows us to form a coherent society and to preserve practices, beliefs and norms across generations. Nobody wants to go against these for fear of shame. Yet we all must act as if we, 'purely exquisitely ourselves', embrace the norms only because we happen to authentically agree with them.

And yet, as we have seen, Spinoza sees the formation of the state and rebellion as stemming from precisely the same cause: the affective power of the crowd over the individual. Of course, there are individuals who rebel, but how many rebels are in fact sustained by the moral approval of a *different* crowd?[33] The queer activist Quentin Crisp made the cutting observation: 'The young always have the same problem – how to rebel and conform at the same time. They have now solved this by defying their parents and copying one another.'[34] Because the young form a crowd, they can create new conformist norms as quickly as they overturn the old ones. In this way they can be rebelliously independent and righteously conformist at the same time. The beauty of this is that it solves the paradox of authenticity. By rebelling, you show your authenticity – you are your own independent person not pandering to the authorities. By conforming, you show that you are (spontaneously, of course) pandering to the *de facto* authority of the crowd, identifying with approved models, showing no treacherous tendencies, and calling forth no punitive coalitions – at least not from your *own* 'cousins'.

But although the desire for glory, born of the thirst for identity, is the core of human sociability, Spinoza regarded it as humanity's original sin. In his strange reading of the Garden of Eden story, Adam falls by 'imitating the affects of the beasts' (E 4p68s). I have argued before, in a book called *The Philosophy of Hope*, that the relevant feature here is the imitation, not the beasts.[35] That is, Adam imitates the beasts only because there is nobody else to imitate – not Eve, because she is not yet distinguished from him.[36] Actually, it is Eve who is first influenced by a beast, the serpent, but Spinoza does not dwell on this detail; he treats Adam and Eve as one, because his point is much more general: *humanity falls by beginning to imitate*. The Fall is the beginning of the search for identity in the model of another. This is precisely the same interpretation that some have given to the story of Hundun.[37]

Consequences of the Fall

Why does Spinoza regard the very condition of human culture and society as a fallen state? We have already seen how the thirst for identity leads naturally to violence. We can now add nuance to this point. This thirst leads to a decline in *reactive* violence but an increase in *proactive* violence. And it is this, the capacity to calculate, organize and institutionalize violence on anywhere up to a continental or even global scale, that is the uniquely haunting quality of our species.

The thirst for identity both drives and is driven by this violent tendency. But, again, an identity resting precariously on the power of the crowd gives little peace even to those who achieve it. The possibility of shifts of power among rival crowds – changings of the guard in the tyranny of the cousins – creates a general sense of anxiety even in those who have achieved a secure and glorious identity. Yu Hua describes the turnings of fate that became common during the Cultural Revolution in China, which became known as 'flipping pancakes': 'everyone was just a pancake sizzling on the griddle, flipped from side to side by the hand of fate. Yesterday's revolutionary became today's counterrevolutionary, just as today's counterrevolutionary would become tomorrow's revolutionary.'[38] Spinoza's age of religious wars had something of the same character. He describes us as being 'like the waves of the sea, driven about by opposing winds' (E 3p59s).

Ultimately, the tendency is always towards self-deception. We have had to evolve a capacity for convincing the crowd that we are not *trying* to conform, rather that we spontaneously, in our authentic character, emulate a model that the crowd finds familiar and praiseworthy. The most efficient way to convince others is to convince ourselves. But the truth is quite otherwise. There is no authentic self. The settlement of the *wu* 吾 upon a *wo* 我 is never decisive and always extrinsic – always guided by external influences and exemplars. Our insatiable appetite for being determined by an identity evolved, in our infancy as a social species, through the power of the crowd to mete out shame and glory.

It is therefore impossible to *seek ourselves* without, perhaps unconsciously, seeking glory. People climb Everest to find themselves, and then they have to tell everyone. They go on retreats to reconnect with their soul and share the results on social media. Spinoza quotes Cicero: 'The best are most led by glory: even philosophers who write treatises on contempt for glory sign their names in them' (E 3def.aff.44). He appends this quotation to a statement that whatever other desire a person has, they *also* have the desire for glory. And he warns that: 'Those who are most believed to be downcast and humble are commonly the most ambitious and envious' (E 3def.aff.29).

Because identity is so precarious an achievement, we go to great lengths to protect it, and this leads to further self-deception. Upton Sinclair once quipped: 'It is difficult to get a man to understand something, when his salary depends upon his not understanding it.'[39] Well, try getting somebody to understand something when their *identity* depends upon not understanding it. If they do not even realize that they are protecting their identity, their mind will confabulate prolifically to explain their resistance to understanding. It will tell itself a story, for example that the source of the proffered understanding is an unreliable creep, a dangerous manipulator. Perhaps, the mind's defence mechanisms will go on, we need to gather together a righteous coalition to deal with this dangerous trickster. The real barrier, of course, is that if the person understood what they were being asked to understand they would not be *themselves* any more. But we are inclined to hide away our own pursuit and defence of identity, burying it under as many conspiracy theories as we need.

Blind to what drives us, we end up in contradictions – what

Spinoza calls a *fluctuation of the spirit* (E 3p17s). We want to be our own independent selves, but our only models for selfhood are found in others. Our ambition cries out for common feeling with others, and yet, turning rivalrous, it drives us into conflict and division:

> each of us, by his nature, wants the others to live according to his temperament; when all alike want this, they are alike an obstacle to one another, and when all wish to be praised, or loved, by all, they hate one another. (E 3p31s)

A state of self-deception and confusion, accompanied by an omnipresent threat of a descent into violence, is reasonably regarded as a state of sin. Spinoza sees all this as following from the original pursuit of identity through emulation, and so the beginnings of emulation are, for him, the Fall.

But what did we fall from? In taking on lapsarian terminology, Spinoza commits himself implicitly to the notion of an *unfallen* state: the state that Christians call *beatitude*. Spinoza is unafraid to use this word. If the Fall begins with the hunger for identity, then beatitude must consist either of *satisfying* this hunger – finding a lasting and secure identity – or *overcoming* it – no longer desiring identity at all. Although Spinoza sometimes toys with the first option, his ultimate philosophical position is to take the second. Beatitude is the exit from identity, an escape from the self.

6.
Beatitude

Beatitude and Eternity

In the Christian conception, beatitude represents a state of perfect happiness, for which humans were originally made by God and from which they were tempted to fall. The imperfect and limited happiness yielded up by worldly things cannot ultimately satisfy creatures who retain a faint notion of this original beatitude.

The early Christian philosopher Boethius, for example, compares the soul of fallen humanity to a caged bird, fed with honey and food. When the bird catches sight of the woods from which she was taken, 'She scatters her food beneath her feet / And all she wants is her woods'.[1] So, we human beings, too, retain a dreamlike image of true happiness – beatitude – beyond the cage of our ordinary notions, which leads us towards fleeting earthly goods.[2] Spinoza's contemporary Blaise Pascal – the French mathematical prodigy, inventor and philosopher, who underwent a profound religious conversion – held firmly to this original Christian vision.[3] 'All men seek happiness,' he wrote. 'There are no exceptions.' And yet (who can deny it?): 'All men complain: princes, subjects, nobles, commoners, old, young, strong, weak, learned, ignorant, healthy, sick, in every country, at every time, of all ages, and all conditions.' So Pascal asks: 'What else does this craving, and this helplessness, proclaim but that there was once in man a true happiness, of which all that now remains is the empty print and trace?'

Spinoza uses the term '*beatitude*' at several points in his *Ethics* (e.g. 2p49s, 4app4, 5pref, 5p42). We have seen that he defines our *highest good* as *self-acquiescence* (E 4p52). We have seen the dangers in pursuing this. Acquiescing in yourself requires you to have a notion of yourself. This notion will have to be sought in some model. But that means emulation, rivalry, ambition, and all the strife and anxiety that come with them. If 'beatitude' and 'highest good' mean the same thing, then Spinoza's identification of the highest good with identity carries over to beatitude and brings all its accompanying problems. It turns out that they do not mean the same thing. Beatitude, for Spinoza no less than for traditional Christians, means the return to a sort of primordial perfection from which we have fallen.

Pascal's Christian view is that 'God alone is man's true good'. Since humanity abandoned God, we have tried to replace him, with 'stars, sky, earth, elements, plants, cabbages, leeks, animals, insects, calves, serpents, fever, plague, war, famine, vice, adultery, incest' – without God, Pascal believed, we are capable of seeing the true good in anything at all, even in our own destruction.[4] Spinoza, also, finds beatitude to lie in God. It is, he asserts, 'nothing other than that acquiescence of the soul [*animi acquiescentia*], which arises from intuitive cognition of God' (E 4app4, O4.432). But his concept of God is highly abstract and philosophical – very different from the loving father of creation described in Scripture and recognized by Christian thinkers like Boethius and Pascal.

It is highly significant that Spinoza, when he moves from discussing the 'highest good' to discussing beatitude, stops using the term *self-acquiescence* and begins to use *acquiescence of the soul*. The *self* drops out and is replaced by the *soul*. We have seen that the Fall, for Spinoza, is a fall into imitation. We fall into the pursuit of identity concretized into some external model. On the other hand, as we have also seen, desire is *metaphysical*: we cannot desire at all without desiring to *be something*. The state of beatitude, of perfectly satisfied desire, must therefore still be framed around a model. It must therefore be a model *without identity*. But that sounds like nonsense. It brings to mind the notion of a being with no qualities, no characteristics, no determinate form at all. It is hard to see what would distinguish that from mere nothingness. Here is where Spinoza's strange and heretical idea of God comes to the rescue.

Beatitude, Spinoza tells us, comes from intuitive knowledge of God. Like some other scholars, I understand this intuitive knowledge, which Spinoza also calls 'intellectual love of God' (E 5p33), to be a form of emulation.[5] We must recall the crucial elements of his theory. Acquiescence is a state of satisfied desire. All desire is a desire for being. Being always means being according to some model. In ordinary human desire, the model is of an ideal self – an aspirational identity. But in beatitude, the model is God. What is special about God is the complete absence of any determinate self or identity.[6] To succeed in emulating God – to reach beatitude – is not to express an exemplary identity; it is to express the complete dissolution of identity. Spinoza, like Zhuangzi, is recommending that we imitate *identitylessness* rather than a model with a distinct identity.[7] To understand this, we must understand what sort of being Spinoza's God is.

Superdeterminacy

Spinoza's definition of God is: 'a being absolutely infinite, that is, a substance comprising infinite attributes, each of which expresses an eternal and infinite essence' (E 1def6). Spinoza's terms, 'substance' and 'attribute', appear to have been drawn from Descartes, the philosophical pioneer, mathematician, physicist and anatomist, whose writings helped to introduce the young Spinoza to the wonders of modern philosophy and science, and who, we have seen, was living in Amsterdam when Spinoza was a child there.[8] Very roughly, a substance is a thing, and an attribute is a property or quality of a thing. But Descartes uses 'attribute' in a more specialized way. He finds the idea of a single thing having multiple attributes nonsensical,[9] since 'attribute', as he uses the term, means a thing's *essential* or *principal* property: the property that tells you *what the thing fundamentally is*. Thought is the attribute of a mind, and extension is the attribute of a body.

But if an attribute tells you *what something fundamentally is* then attributes must be exclusive. To be a mind is not to be a body, and vice versa. So a substance with both thought and extension would have to be different from itself. When Descartes refutes this possibility, it is put to him by an interlocutor who most likely had not thought the matter through. But Spinoza is a philosopher of a different calibre. He, I propose, *welcomes* the consequence that God, as a substance with not only multiple but infinite attributes, is different from himself. This is not the place for a lengthy discourse on Spinoza's metaphysics,[10] but one point at least is relevant to his theory of beatitude.

The point is that Spinoza sees any sort of *determination* as *negation* (Letter 50, G3.240). What he seems to mean, again following Descartes,[11] is that to have any determinate form – a shape, for example – a thing must *fail to exist* in a certain portion of reality. To be pyramid-shaped, a body must exist up to a certain boundary in space, defining a pyramid, and then *fail* to exist *beyond* that boundary. To be purely spiritual, a thing must fail to exist in the physical realm, and to be purely physical it must fail to exist in the spiritual domain. In general, a determinate thing is defined by its *nonexistence* – its negation – as much as its existence: knowing what it is depends on knowing where it fails to exist as much as where it succeeds in existing.

But God, being infinite and absolute, contains no negation (E 1d6expl). To quote the 19th–20th-century British philosopher Harold Joachim, Spinoza conceives of God 'as absolutely positive because absolutely real: as excluding all negation from his being'.[12] God cannot fail to exist anywhere. He must be both spiritual *and* material: possessing the attributes of both thought and (physical) extension (E 2p1–2), and all other possible attributes there might be. The crucial point is that this does not result in an *undetermined* God – a God that has no determinate characteristics at all. While some philosophers have believed in the possibility of a God with no determinations, a being beyond all qualities and characteristics, Spinoza does not.[13] Moreover, as the Sufi philosopher Ibn 'Arabī argues, such a God would still suffer the negation of *failing to exist determinately*.[14] Rather, an absolutely infinite being, devoid of all negation, must be *determined in every possible way*.

My term for this is 'superdeterminacy', distinct from the word 'indeterminacy', which conveys an absence rather than an abundance of determination.[15] *Superdeterminacy* is my name for the peculiar property belonging to Spinoza's God, of existing in every possible way – with every possible determination. Not only must God exist as both spiritual and physical; he must exist as you, as me, as this mountain, as that valley, as the USS *Abraham Lincoln*, and as each flower in the vase on my dining table, as well as the vase and the table themselves. Ibn 'Arabī puts the point very directly: 'Whosoever is distinguished from a delimited thing is delimited by not being identical with that delimited thing.'[16] A being that is in no way delimited – free of all negation – must therefore be identical with each and every thing. Spinoza comes close to stating this explicitly in the following passage:

> since the divine nature has absolutely infinite attributes [. . .], each of which moreover expresses an infinite essence in its own kind, therefore infinite[17] in infinite modes (i.e. everything that can fall under an infinite intellect) must necessarily follow from it. (E 1p16d)

The reasoning leads to the conclusion that God is identical to each and every possible thing.

Distinguish the idea of superdeterminacy carefully from the doctrine that God is the *aggregate* of all beings. The latter view is sometimes referred to as 'pantheism' and has been ascribed to Spinoza as well as Ibn 'Arabī.[18] It is misleading. As the scholar Syed Muhammad Naquib al-Attas points out, for Ibn 'Arabī 'there is no such thing as "aggregation of *existents*", as God is *the* only existent'.[19] Ibn 'Arabī's view, which I believe Spinoza shares, is that God is identical to *each* ordinary thing, not to the aggregate composed of *all* of them.

This again carries the outrageous implication that God differs from himself. God is you entirely, and God is me entirely, but I am not you, so in some sense God is not God. In other words, Spinoza violates the same fundamental Aristotelian principle of identity that we found Zhuangzi to be violating in Chapter 3. Descartes, we saw, cannot understand the idea of a substance with multiple attributes, holding to the principle that: 'to be both the same thing and not the same thing – that is, something different – is a contradiction.'[20] It is not necessarily a contradiction, but it certainly violates a logical principle that many regard as fundamental.[21] Giving up that principle might be intellectually uncomfortable at first, but it is necessary for understanding the concept of superdeterminacy, which, I hold, is the only way to make proper sense of Spinoza's idea of God.

The Beatific Soul

The ethical consequences of rejecting the Aristotelian position on identity are the same as those found in Zhuangzi.[22] God does not have any single determinate being. He / she / they / it is, rather, the indifferent affirmation of every possible determination. To emulate God is, therefore, to likewise not be restricted to any determination of being. Of course, you have certain qualities, and you take on different characteristics and play different roles at different times. The point of beatitude is that none of these defines you. Beatific being is supple and can endure any changes in determinate qualities. It is superdeterminate and cannot be exhaustively defined.

The *soul* in which the beatific person acquiesces is different from any *self*. Beatitude means understanding your being as the expression, not of some determinate identity or exemplar, but rather of God's superdeterminate being. The less attached you are to any particular determination – the more readily you can flow from form to form, being carried along by the endless transformations – the less troubled you are by external things. You are more at peace with the world, which is nothing more than the endless expression of God's superdeterminacy through the taking of every possible determinate form, of which there is no end.

The *self* in self-acquiescence, which Spinoza misleadingly calls the *highest* good, is a mere *wo* 我 – one particular determination out of a possible infinity. The *soul* in the acquiescence of soul, which Spinoza calls beatitude and which is above the 'highest' good, is the *wu* 吾 – the indissoluble portion of being that resists absorption into any identity.[23] Beatitude is the capacity to embrace this *being prior to any identity*, which is capable of taking on all manner of forms but never fully *identifying* with any of them – or at least never to the exclusion of other distinct possibilities.

Beatitude is returning into the bosom of God. This can be seen in the odd way Spinoza identifies the state of beatitude with the *intellectual love of God*, which he also identifies with *God's love for human beings* (E 5p36c). How can *your love for God* be the same as *God's love for human beings*? My explanation, which I give in detail in *The Philosophy of Hope*, is in terms of God's superdeterminacy.[24] Beatitude means escaping confinement to any determinate identity and returning to the primitive superdeterminate being, of which all determinate identities are inadequate expressions. It is the recovery of a primitive perfect state – superdeterminacy – from which we fell into the pursuit of determinate identity. In this state, the beatified are really at one with God, so that their love and God's love become identical. Moreover, their love for God is the same as God's love for each human being – or, what is the same, their love for each human being – since each human being is an expression of God's superdeterminate nature.

When Spinoza writes that the beatified person 'never ceases to be but obtains true acquiescence of the soul always [*semper*]' (E 5p42s), the reasoning is similar to that found in the 'death stories' of the Zhuangzi.[25] To die is to be transformed into something that is *not yourself* – into what no longer counts as you. But in the state of beatitude, *anything* can count as 'you'.[26] When your being is the expression of superdeterminacy, there can be no death, only change.[27]

In the same passage, Spinoza contrasts the beatified person with the ignorant person, who is 'agitated by external causes'. For this person, 'as soon as he ceases to be acted on, he ceases to be'. We are inclined to think of causes in the paradigm of billiard balls colliding, but one important type of cause identified by Descartes is an *example*.[28] What Spinoza appears to be saying is that the non-beatified person identifies herself with an external exemplar and ceases to be as soon as she no longer emulates that exemplar. The beatified, by contrast, takes superdeterminacy as her exemplar. She has no identity, and nothing to lose in the endless flux of transformation. She is at one with the flux.

A Many-Splendoured Thing

This might all feel very abstract, but the practical meaning of Spinozist beatitude can perhaps be illustrated more tangibly through Han Suyin's grand meditation on the Eurasian experience, *A Many-Splendoured Thing*. This novel, one of my favourites, provides a most direct and concrete application of the anti-identitarian philosophy that we have explored. 'Han Suyin' is the pen name of Rosalie Matilda Kuanghu Chou (1916/7–2012), a doctor and novelist, who had a Chinese father and a Belgian mother. Born in China (near Henan province, where Zhuangzi is said to have originated), she lived in Belgium, Britain, Hong Kong, Malaya, India and Switzerland, and wrote of her experiences in all these places as a Eurasian. By the strict racial categories established during the colonial era, a Eurasian is two different things at once. 'Han Suyin' is also the name of the main character in the semi-fictional story of *A Many-Splendoured Thing*. Thus, Han Suyin is superdeterminate in at least two senses: both Asian and European, both real and fictional.

In the novel, a British man, soon to become her lover, tells Suyin: 'You can't be both East and West at the same time. You have to choose between the two.'[29] While other people are torn between different possible actions, Suyin reflects that she is torn between 'different ways of existence'. She is, she laments, 'Tiresias, Tiresias to the core, if a core is left to a being so much like Peer Gynt's onion as I'.[30] In Greek myth, the prophet Tiresias lives first as a man, then as a woman, then as a man again, transformed by the goddess Hera. After he dies, he retains his gift of prophecy and is able to communicate with the living, hovering between the realms of life and death. He serves as Suyin's emblem of superdeterminacy. The determinate people around her, entrenched in their various national and political identities, constantly call upon her to identify herself. Is she East or West? Communist or capitalist? Suyin keeps dodging these questions, gliding evasively among the identity-traps that others set for her in their anxiety. They are anxious that she confirms the categories in terms of which their own identities are defined. Layers of identity are peeled off her like 'Peer Gynt's onion', revealing no core but only endlessly more layers.[31]

In the beginning, Suyin suffers from her Tiresian corelessness: 'the thousand tangles in my brain, the thousand ways of explaining one thing, the mischief of words and their many-faced interpretations'.[32] But by the end of the novel she appears to have embraced the absence as a source of power, a power capable of carrying her through grief and loss:

> In my empty enchanted hands I hold fabulous treasure; the immense nothingness of heaven, the vacancy of space, and time's fleet magic. Look how it has transformed me. For I am now crowned with negation, mantled with absence, throned on nothingness, empress of exceeding glory, the splendour and wealth of love and death.[33]

I believe that this passage should be understood in terms of Daoist philosophy, since throughout the book Suyin declares herself a Daoist and makes Daoist-sounding pronouncements such as: 'A person with awareness can know many things without having to incur them,'[34] and: 'We cannot stop the eternal insubstantial change, demand a conclusion, fix with a name, presuppose an end; [. . .] There never is an end. Only a way.'[35] The nothingness from which Suyin proposes to draw her power is Daoist in nature: not a void but, as Ellen Chen puts it, a 'dynamic emptiness', which 'gives rise to the richly variegated beings of the world'.[36] Nothingness, in other words, means *being that is nothing in particular*. It is a sort of ultimate being that is manifested in richly variegated forms but is exhaustively defined by none of them – the *wu* 吾 that can be expressed in any *wo* 我 but retains its residue beyond all of them. It is Hundun.

It is, in other words, not an 'emptiness' but really a fullness of being beyond identity. Suyin is able to inhabit various characters, forms and roles without being identified by any of them – 'to know many things without having to incur them'. This allows her to endure all the vicissitudes of life. This strategy of endurance is very different from a strategy that aims to preserve a definite identity against all interference and transformation – the sort of immutable eternity celebrated in some ancient Greek thought and informing the whole Western religious and philosophical tradition.[37] Daoist eternity is, by contrast, premised on an infinite capacity for transformation.[38] This is the sort of eternity Suyin grasps. Rather than fixing an identity for herself and trying to hold out against change, she embraces it by living without attachment to any single identity. The novel ends:

> I have dreamed a wonderful dream to shield me from the night, and the breath of heaven itself cannot blow my dream away.
>
> I have dreamed a wonderful dream; of life, and love and death, of laughter and tears, and good and ill, and all these things which are equal under Heaven, which equalizes all things.[39]
>
> A wonderful dream, my many-splendoured thing.[40]

Her taste of beatitude lies in entering into the identitylessness of eternal transformation.

Suyin's 'many-splendoured thing' is of course a reference to love in Shakespeare's Sonnet 116. But Suyin's meaning goes deeper than that. Suyin herself is the many-splendoured thing. This is why she can endure any change without ceasing to be herself. Each of the new forms she takes on, in a life already full of loss and dislocation as new fissures open in the world – the start of China's revolution and the long 'handover' of Hong Kong – is as much herself as the last. Suyin is an imitation of Spinoza's superdeterminate God and thus, to that extent, beatific and eternal.

The Buddhist No-Self

The ideal of beatitude, which we have seen in Zhuangzi and Spinoza, can be clarified further when we compare it to modern interpretations of Buddhism. When I bring up this idea of finding beatitude by escaping the self in casual conversation, people are often inclined to relate it to Buddhist ideas. The relation, however, is far from clear. Jay Garfield, a scholar of Buddhist thought, wrote a book called *Losing Ourselves: Learning to Live Without a Self.* You might expect it to advocate for a similar philosophy that is against identity. In fact, it promotes nearly the exact opposite.[41]

The self that Garfield enjoins us to lose is what the Madhyamaka Buddhist scholar Candakīrti (*c.* 600–*c.* 650) and other related thinkers know as *ātman*: 'that which is always the subject, never the object', 'that which persists through life despite changes in body and mind, and which even persists beyond death and in transmigration'.[42] This appears to line up with the notion of *wu* 吾 – the portion of your being beyond any specific self with which you might identify. Garfield draws broadly on arguments from Buddhist thinkers to show that this *ātman* does not exist. More than this, Garfield warns, the illusion of it 'obscures our own identities from us'.[43] He hopes to clear away the notion of *ātman* to make space for us to embrace our true identities as what he calls *persons*: 'To be a person is to play a role; the person you are is constituted by the multiple roles you play, including family roles, professional roles, roles in networks of friends, and political roles.'[44]

Garfield observes that your *person* is a sort of fiction – constructed by your whole community and not just yourself. This corresponds to how I have been describing identity throughout this book. Identity is your reputation in the eyes of others alongside your notion of yourself, with the two always reacting upon each other.

Garfield argues that although your *person* is fictional, it is nevertheless a fact. He makes this point by way of a dubious etymology, tracing the words 'fact' and 'fiction' to a common root in the Latin '*fingere*'. I think, rather, that 'fact' belongs to the quite different root '*facere*', and the fiction of identity – the person that you are – really is merely fictional.[45] But, since Garfield has denied the existence of *ātman* – the portion of your being that resists absorption into any of the identities you adopt or have imposed upon you – he is forced to claim reality for identity, since there is nothing else in which your being could consist. If Garfield's arguments against the existence of *ātman* work also against *wu* 吾, that would be devastating for the philosophy of Zhuangzi and Spinoza. Fortunately, I believe that his argument misses the mark.

In order to bring to mind our innate notion of *ātman*, Garfield presents a thought experiment. First, he asks us to imagine we are given the power to *have somebody else's body* for a short period. Garfield chooses Usain Bolt in his prime; he wants to experience the feeling of running 100 metres in 9.6 seconds. He clarifies that 'in developing this desire, I do not want to *be* Usain Bolt. [. . .] I want to be *me*, Jay, with Usain Bolt's body, so that I can enjoy what Usain Bolt experiences.'[46] Next, he asks us to imagine having the mind of Stephen Hawking, 'for long enough to understand general relativity and quantum gravity'.[47] Again: 'this is not a desire to *be* Stephen Hawking, but to be *me*, enjoying his mind.' This thought experiment is supposed to show that what we think of as our *self* – our notion of *ātman* – is to be identified neither with our body nor our mind, since we can allegedly imagine having a different body and mind to our own. From this point, it is not difficult for Garfield to show that the notion is vacuous. If neither our body nor our mind answers to this notion of *ātman*, then to what exactly does it refer? Nothing else we can point to seems to qualify, so *ātman* appears to be a wholly empty concept.

I am always suspicious of thought experiments, and this one contains a few tricks. In the Stephen Hawking case, Garfield's language tempts us to imagine him having a certain *part* of Hawking's mind – his understanding of theoretical physics. But he claims to be discussing the possibility of having the *whole* of Hawking's mind. That would mean having all of Hawking's memories and keeping none of his own. Keeping his own, after all, would mean not *having Hawking's mind* but rather *having a fusion of Hawking's mind with his own*. Simply having Hawking's mind would mean having all and only the sensations, experiences, thoughts, memories, beliefs, etc., of Hawking, which would presumably mean not even knowing who Jay Garfield is.[48] I am not convinced that I understand what it would be for Garfield to have Hawking's mind without simply becoming Hawking.

For those who believe the mind to be the body, or a part of the body such as the brain, the same will apply in the Usain Bolt case. But even if you believe the mind to be distinct from the body, as long as you believe that all sensations and memories occur and are stored in the brain, you will have to suppose that when Garfield *has Bolt's body* he will have no idea that he is Garfield in possession of Bolt's body. Bolt's brain, after all, does not contain any traces of Garfield's experiences or memories. To have Bolt's body is to have only Bolt's experiences and memories. Again, it is difficult to see how losing all the contents of Garfield's own brain and taking on all of Bolt's could count as *being Garfield with Bolt's body* rather than just *being Bolt*.

Garfield might reply that this is precisely his point. The notion of *ātman* is empty, so these scenarios are not really conceivable. But the purpose of the thought experiment was to help identify our innate notion of *ātman*. If the scenarios make no sense, then they fail to illuminate the notion. A more reasonable inference to draw from their incoherence is that our idea of *ātman* is not what Garfield takes it to be. It is not a notion of something distinct from the mind and the body. Rather, it stands for our awareness that our mind and body are broader than any 'person' in Garfield's sense: they always can be different from the 'person' they have become, and thus no 'person' can exhaustively define them.

Garfield rejects *ātman* in order to deny that we are anything beyond the identities we construct and have constructed for us. But thinking that you are more than those identities does not require you to believe you are some strange ethereal substance capable of 'having' somebody else's mind or body. It only requires you to believe, as discussed in Chapter 1, that any answer to the question of what *defines* you is infinitely revisable. Garfield identifies Usain Bolt's body by its running speed and Stephen Hawking's mind by its comprehension of theoretical physics. Bolt and Hawking may or may not agree that these are the things that define them. Even if they do, they might change their opinion later on. For example, Bolt might start off feeling very alienated from his body as it ages but then come to accept it as the same old body, just differently constituted. Or Hawking might start off thinking that his scientific knowledge and extraordinary abilities define the fundamental character of his mind but then come later to decide that no, it is something else—his personality or the unique palette of his imagination, or his courage and inner strength. Any identity by which we try to define them, even a much more detailed and nuanced one than *runner* or *physicist*, will leave certain things out – things that, had they been emphasized instead, would have defined a different identity. Nurturing these other elements would transform the body and mind.

In short, we all carry in us an element of the superdeterminacy of God – that is, of Spinoza's God, which is more a metaphysical principle expressed through the world than any sort of supernatural creator, and could be identified with the way, or *dao* 道 (as discussed in Chapter 1). The way to appreciate your own superdeterminacy is not by contemplating imponderable scenarios of body- or mind-swapping. It is by recognizing that no identity that anyone attaches to you, even you yourself, is ever complete or final. This invincible resistance to identity signals the presence of the *wu* 吾 – an endlessly transforming potential wrapping up every possible being, a Hundun-Wonton, rather than the reified void that Garfield identifies with *ātman*. Acquiescing in this *wu* 吾, resisting all attempts at capture into the various *wo* 我, sailing skilfully between the myriad *persons* with which the world tries to ensnare us – this is the means to Spinozist beatitude.

PART THREE
Girard

7.
Postmodern Paris to Silicon Valley

Existentialism and the Liberation of Paris

Introducing René Girard's era is difficult and perhaps unnecessary, since it still lies in living memory. Born on Christmas Day in 1923, Girard lived until 2015, witnessing the development of both the theories and the technologies that saturate modern life.[1] In Paris he breathed the air of postwar existentialism, as we will see below. At Johns Hopkins University, he engaged with poststructuralism, deconstruction and other trends in literary theory. At Stanford University, adjacent to Silicon Valley, in the United States, he was surrounded by the earliest experiments with social media and even taught one of the world's most politically active tech billionaires. In all these philosophical movements and social developments, questions of identity ruled supreme. Girard's research, which ranged from a study of the representation of desire in the novel to a discussion of apocalyptic literature and its relation to globalization, war and terrorism, is thus tied together by a concern with our striving for identity.[2] Reading down to the core of his wide-ranging studies of literature, anthropology, religion and violence we find, at its heart, a similar philosophy to the one we discovered in Zhuangzi and Spinoza.

Girard always denied being a philosopher, on the grounds that he rejected 'abstract speculation' in favour of 'what is'.[3] But philosophy as I have defined it – as a certain way of looking at life and the world, aiming at an ability to navigate life wisely – is surely found in his pages.[4] Indeed, trained as a medieval archivist, Girard is most famous for a theory of scapegoating, which might be regarded as anthropological. However, we will largely focus instead on his theory of desire, and how scapegoating connects to it – which has profound philosophical implications. In fact, what spurred on Girard's intellectual journey was one of the most iconic philosophical movements: existentialism. This is, therefore, where we begin our exploration of Girard's thoughts on identity.

Girard came of age during the Nazi occupation of France during the Second World War and then its liberation. The dominant philosophical voice at the time was that of the arch-existentialist, Jean-Paul Sartre. Girard reports that Sartre's 1943 book, *Being and Nothingness*, was the first philosophical book he understood.[5] Together with his lifelong partner and collaborator, Simone de Beauvoir, Sartre exercised a profound influence on postwar French philosophy, and on the young Girard.

Sartre and Beauvoir centred their philosophical message on the slogan 'existence precedes essence', which Sartre explains as meaning that 'man as existentialists conceive of him cannot be defined [. . .] because to begin with he is nothing'. The stark consequence is that 'man is nothing other than what he makes of himself. This is the first principle of existentialism.'[6] Of course, we do not choose our parents, the bodies we are born with, our appearance, or the preconceptions others have of us. But what we do with this raw material is our choice. Nor can we be guided in our choices by any objective values, since there are none. 'If God does not exist,' writes Sartre (and he assumes the premise), 'we will encounter no values or orders that can legitimate our conduct.'[7] And, most importantly for us, existentialism also denies that we have any intrinsic *identity* to determine our choices.

Arguably the chief bewitchment against which existentialism fights is the temptation to let identity make life choices for you, forgetting that it is ultimately you who decides on your identity. As a historian of this movement, Sarah Bakewell, puts it: 'In a reversal of Descartes's "I think therefore I am", Sartre argues, in effect, "I am nothing, therefore I am free".' I am 'nothing' in the sense that, although I inherit 'personality traits, tendencies, limitations, relics of past hurts and so on, all pinning me down to an identity, [. . .] none of these things can define me at all'.[8] These character traits cannot define me unless I *choose* for them to define me, in which case it is really *me defining myself by selecting those qualities I identify with* and not *those qualities defining me*.

In a radio interview, Sartre related his core philosophy to the event of France's liberation, which had just occurred at the time: 'There is no traced-out path to lead man to his salvation; he must constantly invent his own path. But, to invent it, he is free, responsible, without excuse, and every hope lies within him.'[9] The colossal destructiveness of the war – not just of lives and cities, but of people's faith in the old social and political institutions, meant that the world needed something new. Sartre's encouraging message was that we all have the power to invent ourselves *ex nihilo*. Existentialism is sometimes regarded as a depressing philosophy, on account of its denial of objective values and meaning in the world. But in the interview quoted, Sartre's tone is bracing. Europe's gods had failed, nations, churches, ideologies, institutions and philosophers had guided humanity to disaster, but now people were free to decide what to be and what sort of world to create, unencumbered by the guides of the past. It is worth dwelling for a moment on how European thinking had arrived at this point from the cultural situation of Spinoza's time.

Decolonization and New Identities

This new existentialist philosophy suited a world in which entire states had disappeared, new states had come into existence, new institutions had to be built from no precedent, and ideologies that had recently energized populations had yielded disaster. There was room for this attitude in the creation of new global institutions such as the United Nations and the Bretton Woods system. But it appears perhaps most directly in the context of decolonization – the dismantling of the European empires that were being built while Spinoza was writing in the Dutch Republic. Philosophy needed to speak to this, and the existentialists were willing to try. Sartre wrote an enthusiastic preface to Frantz Fanon's *The Wretched of the Earth* (1963). Originating from the colonized Caribbean island of Martinique, the psychiatrist and philosopher addresses all colonized peoples – or at least all those colonized by Europe. He enjoins them to throw off any cringing traces of European identity.[10] 'The European game,' Fanon declares, 'has finally ended; we must find something different.'[11] What this 'something different' is to be, he does not say. But he is clear that it will be a new creation: 'The human condition, plans for mankind, and collaboration between men in those tasks which increase the sum total of humanity are new problems, which demand true inventions.'[12] The 'Third World' has to start 'a new history of man'.[13]

But how to start it? And who is this 'man' whose history is to be written anew? The novel by Indonesian author Mochtar Lubis, *Twilight in Jakarta*, which was also published in 1963, presented the more anguished side of decolonized peoples, as they took up the radical responsibility to create new systems and values, neither guided nor encumbered by the past. Lubis wrote the novel in the 1950s while he was being held under house arrest by the newly formed, independent Indonesian government. Throughout the novel, a study group meets to discuss fundamental problems of Indonesian identity. Every possibility is considered. Should Indonesia follow the example of communist China, or would this involve sacrificing its characteristically democratic culture? Can there really be a *national* Indonesian culture, including the *gamelan*, the Sundanese *angklung* and lute, 'the *serimpi* dance of Central Java, the dances of Bali, the plate and handkerchief dances of Sumatra, the *cakalélé* of the Moluccas, the *pakaréné* of Sulawesi, and so on'?[14] Is Islam the key to spiritual uplift in Indonesia, or would that be the mere imitation of an Arabic model? Is Indonesia's cultural and political identity grounded in the national ideal of *Pancasila*? One character even proposes Sartre's existentialism as an answer to the question of Indonesian identity: 'an Indonesian must first of all realize that he exists, and that his fate is in his own hands. That his life is not determined by his family, not by the economic system, but that he has enough inner strength to determine himself.'[15]

In a broader sense, all members of the study group are facing the condition defined by Sartre. Having overthrown their colonial oppressors, they see that 'there is no traced-out path' for them, that they must invent their own path. They can follow the routes of others, but the choice to do so would still have to be made spontaneously. In *Twilight in Jakarta*, independence has been achieved and the abundance of choice has become a source of anxiety. The study group ends up dispersing with no definite resolutions, only abstract platitudes: 'They took leave of each other with mutual assurances of cooperation in the cause of the people's cultural uplift and the destruction of the residue of feudalistic cultural influences.'[16]

The ascendancy of existentialism in many countries around the world reveals an age of a collapsing identity regime. The regime of racial and national identity that had provided so much of the ideological background to the World Wars disintegrated, as people, individuals and nations found a new freedom to ask the question of *who they are*. The old answers had led to violence and oppression. Thus, the world needed a new vision of identity.

Enlightenment and Counter-Enlightenment

The identity regime of the early twentieth century had itself grown out of the failure of another project: the Enlightenment era, which followed the time of Spinoza's writing. The project of the Enlightenment had been to unite humanity into a broad cosmopolitan identity, grounded on notions of a universal human nature and abstract reason. The Enlightenment movement was dominated by urban bourgeois intellectuals like Spinoza and, for all its universalist rhetoric, left many people feeling excluded.[17] This proved one of its greatest weaknesses.

An emblem of this weakness is the figure of the eighteenth-century Swiss philosopher Jean-Jacques Rousseau, who came to Paris in the hope of joining the sophisticated set of Enlightenment *philosophes* but, being foreign and low-born, was never fully accepted into the club. The Indian author Pankaj Mishra, seeking the philosophical sources of contemporary global conflicts, identifies Rousseau as an early exemplar of the embittered, anti-elitist sentiment that continues to this day to fuel political movements that challenge the legacy of the Enlightenment and highlight its limitations. According to Mishra, Rousseau 'was the prototype of the man who feels himself, despite his obvious success, to be at the bottom of the social pyramid, and knows that he can never fit into the existing order'.[18] He represents 'the quintessential inner experience of modernity for most people: the uprooted outsider in the commercial metropolis, aspiring for a place in it, and struggling with complex feelings of envy, fascination, revulsion and rejection'.[19]

Rousseau was enthusiastically read by members of the German Romantic movement.[20] One of the greatest was Johann Gottfried Herder, who, like Rousseau, travelled to Paris, filled initially with 'a fervent desire to wear the French identity of a sociable man and be a charming salon wit'. This then 'shaded into premature and acute disappointment', as Herder also failed to achieve insider status in the fashionable salons.[21] Like Rousseau, he reacted by developing a defensive contempt for the society that had turned its nose up at him, claiming a superior identity grounded in everything the French cosmopolitans lacked: rootedness, connection to the *Volk*, an earthy, organic language, a relationship with folk traditions. Such was the origin of the grand nineteenth-century obsession with *national culture*, expressed in all the compiling of folktales, invention of national traditions,[22] and attempts to create nationalistic styles in music, painting and literature associated with this period.

And yet, as Mishra points out, nationalistic identities of this sort never escape the original inferiority complex that gave rise to them.[23] What led the nationalists to reject Enlightenment cosmopolitanism was an envious desire to possess the sort of self-assured high status enjoyed by the cosmopolitans. In emphasizing their differences from the Enlightenment *philosophes*, figures like Rousseau and Herder were really trying to emulate them: to show that just as the *philosophes* had no need of them, they likewise had no need of the *philosophes*.

As we know today, this sort of nationalistic, culturally chauvinistic identity failed to bring peace, and nowhere was this clearer than in the war-ravaged world of the young René Girard – the world in which Sartre's anti-identitarian message found such resonance. When people's attempts to find their identity as sophisticated cosmopolitans were met with snobbery and exclusion, they turned to defining their identity in opposition to those who had rejected them. Yet this performative rejection was grounded in a suppressed desire for emulation, thus pulling in two directions. While Sartre was pursuing his own radical line of escape, Girard began developing his own theory of how the pursuit of identity led to this paradoxical result.

Mimetic Desire

Girard first developed his theory of identity and desire through an accidental encounter with literature. Originally trained as a medieval archivist at the prestigious École des Chartres, in Paris, Girard moved to the United States in 1947 to study for a PhD in History at Indiana University.[24] At that time, as he would later recall, 'I was more of a historian. I was not at all a literary man.'[25] However, Indiana needed somebody to teach French, and Girard ended up in charge of a class studying novels by authors including Balzac, Stendhal and Proust. Girard had not read these novels himself; he was, he remembers, 'just a few pages ahead of [his] students' and struggled to know what to say. He decided to look for something that the great novels had in common, which turned out to be the theory of desire that would become the foundation of his philosophy.

The young history student could not have known it then, but this idea would launch Girard into a lifelong study of the deep roots of human culture, archaic religion and the meaning of the Christian revelation. Although his work would cover a vast range of topics and sources – he produced studies of Greek tragedy, Victorian-era anthropology, the Bible, comparative religion, Shakespeare, anorexia, the Prussian general Carl von Clausewitz, and even the ancient texts of Vedic India[26] – he never lost his archivist's eye for detail, probing texts forensically to discover what they reveal about the cultures that produced them, and – importantly – what they try to conceal.

His first book, *Mensonge romantique et Vérité romanesque* (The Romantic Lie and Novelistic Truth), developed his theory of desire through an encounter with the novels of Cervantes, Stendhal, Flaubert, Proust and Dostoevsky, expanding beyond the French canon that he had encountered by accident. The book was published in 1961 (the English translation has a slightly different title: *Deceit, Desire, and the Novel*). The *romantic lie* is Girard's name for the idea that our selves are our own individual creation: 'the emanation of a serene subjectivity, the creation *ex nihilo* of a quasi-divine ego'.[27]

'The romantic lie' is an implicit attack on the Sartrean idea that we are free to make ourselves into whatever we want to be. The phrase that Girard uses, '*ex nihilo*' – *from nothing* – echoes Sartre's claim given in a public lecture in 1946, 'Existentialism is a Humanism', that when we make the choices that end up defining us we 'cannot find anything to rely on – neither within nor without' and 'have neither behind us, nor before us, in the luminous realm of values, any means of justification or excuse'. Even if we find some sign to guide us, Sartre goes on, 'man interprets the sign as he pleases and [. . .] is therefore without any support or help, condemned at all times to invent man'.[28] We can, as Sartre knows well, be guided by a church, a crowd, an advisor, an influencer, but only if we *choose* to be so guided. Behind any guided choice there is a choice of a guide, and, on pain of an infinite regress, Sartre holds, the chain must bottom out at an ultimately unguided choice – an act of pure, spontaneous will.

For Girard, this idea is a romantic lie, by which he means an attractive illusion – a lie we tell ourselves, which flatters our pride by obscuring the real source of our identity and desires. Such a lie ascribes to us a 'quasi-divine' power of creating ourselves from nothing. In fact, Girard suggests, self-invention is never *ex nihilo*; it must always begin from an external model. The novels he examines reveal would-be Sartrean heroes – figures who think they are creating themselves spontaneously: Julien Sorel in Stendhal's *Red and Black*, Emma Bovary in Flaubert's *Madame Bovary*, the unnamed narrator of Dostoevsky's *The Underground Man*.

Reading the novels closely, Girard finds that all these figures are in fact driven to emulate some external model. Julien Sorel is inspired by Napoleon, Emma Bovary by the heroes of the romance novels she reads, and the 'underground man' by a military officer who humiliates him and about whom he develops an unhealthy obsession (more on this in the next chapter). In truth, Girard contends, these characters are no different from Cervantes's Don Quixote, who strives in all things to emulate the hero of chivalric legend, Amadis of Gaul. But whereas Quixote is conscious of his emulative striving, the others are oblivious to it. They fall for the romantic lie – believing that they are purely autonomous, in denial about the fact that they have modelled themselves on others. The unwelcome fact behind the romantic lie is what Girard calls the *novelistic truth*.

The key to the novelistic truth is Girard's idea of *mimetic desire*. Like Zhuangzi and Spinoza, Girard holds that our desires originally arise from a fundamental drive to emulate some model. 'Mimesis' comes from the ancient Greek word μίμησις (*mīmēsis*), which can mean 'imitate', 'emulate' or 'represent'. Girard uses 'mimetic desire' to refer to desire arising from the urge to *be like* somebody else – whether real or fictional: a *mimetic model*. All desire is guided by models even if, blinded by the romantic lie, we are in denial about this fact.

Conflict and Scapegoating

Deceit, Desire, and the Novel took Girard out of history studies and into the world of literary criticism. In the year it was published, he became a Professor of Romance Languages at Johns Hopkins University in Baltimore and spent the next two decades teaching and travelling between Johns Hopkins and the State University of New York in Buffalo. But his philosophic theories took his ideas to places that reached far beyond literary studies.

His next major book, *Violence and the Sacred* (1972), presented a theory of archaic religion and ritual sacrifice, drawing on anthropology and a comparative study of ancient Greek tragedy and mythology.[29] Early anthropologists had treated ritual sacrifice as the epitome of human unreason: the wilful destruction of precious resources, undertaken to appease imaginary deities or powers. Girard uses his mimetic theory to uncover a hidden and frightening logic behind the institution. In his theory, ritual sacrifice is a symbolic reenactment of a collective murder, dimly remembered through mythic narratives as the moment a community was brought together and rescued from destruction. Girard's hypothesis is that both the destruction and the rescue were very real, although they take on a false and magical aspect in mythic memory. The mimetic theory can explain what really happened. We will find his story familiar, having already seen versions of it in Zhuangzi and Spinoza.

Again, it begins with the pursuit of identity – with the craving for identity leading to the search for external models:

> Once his basic needs are satisfied (indeed, sometimes even before), man is subject to intense desires, though he may not know precisely for what. The reason is that he desires *being*, something he himself lacks and which some other person seems to possess. The subject thus looks to that other person to inform him of what he should desire in order to acquire that being. If the model, who is apparently already endowed with superior being, desires some object, the object must surely be capable of conferring an even greater plenitude of being.[30]

Again, the core insight is that we do not know precisely what we want until we know what it is we are trying to be, and this leads us to look to others to model being for us. Wanting to be like these mimetic models, we come to want the same things they want, developing what Spinoza calls *emulation*, as we saw in Chapter 4.

This craving for being and pursuit of emulative or mimetic models leads to dissatisfaction, rivalry and violence. Since our desires are imitated from others, we end up coveting what others prize and becoming rivals to each other. We want others to imitate our desires, since we want to be like our models and thus to be models ourselves. Yet when others do imitate our desires and begin to covet what we have, we treat them as adversaries and warn them off. 'Man and his desires thus perpetually transmit contradictory signals.'[31] Because the romantic lie prevents us from seeing our truly mimetic nature, we are trapped in a contradiction from which we do not know how to escape. This is profoundly frustrating, and we have nowhere else to direct our frustration but onto our rivals, who take the blame for the trap our desire has led us into. Once violence has emerged, it too is subject to mimesis, spreading contagiously. Communities are led into conflict as if by hypnosis. But how, if we are so prone to conflict, are we able to live at all in peaceful societies, under common rules and norms?

To explain this, Girard invokes a mechanism very similar to the one we found Alexandre Matheron (Girard's contemporary) presenting as implicit in Spinoza: When conflict and violence become sufficiently intense, imitation can lead a whole community to spontaneously concentrate their enmity upon a single individual – the scapegoat. If one person imitates another in hating a third, more and more people will be drawn to imitate this common hatred, until the whole community has polarized against a single despised individual or small group. Since this unfortunate victim becomes the focus of the whole community's ill will, killing the victim, in Girard's view, temporarily brings to the community a cathartic feeling and sense of unity: 'Collective murder restores calm, in dramatic contrast to the hysterical paroxysms that preceded it.'[32] Girard calls this the 'scapegoat mechanism' and insists that it really does work, not because the collective murder appeases the gods or washes the community clean of its sins, but because it vents the rivalrous frustrations of the community and allows it to experience a temporary peace.

Girard finds evidence of this original murder behind every community, buried deep within mythology. Myths, he argues, preserve the memory of the original killing, although in a distorted and fantastical form, for example as stories about mysterious figures who die at the hands of the community and then miraculously return to rescue it from danger. Since the murder brings peace, the community mistakenly assumes that the victim must have been the original cause of all its strife, and it is imaginatively ascribed all manner of magical powers to explain how this could be. When peace seems miraculously restored after the killing, this too is traced to the supernatural powers assigned to the scapegoat. These magical explanations emerge because the real source of the community's strife – mimetic desire – is obscured behind the romantic lie. Ritual sacrifice is the practical version of this distorted memory of the original murder. Although the objects sacrificed can be animals, vegetables, wine or even stones, Girard maintains that these are all symbolic surrogates for human victims, since ritual sacrifice originally evolved from the attempt to recreate the scapegoat effect when the inexorable workings of mimetic desire, sometime after the original murder, drive the community back into rivalry and strife.

Girard believed that all human institutions have their origin in sacrifice. Towards the end of *Violence and the Sacred*, he concludes:

> All religious rituals spring from the surrogate victim, and all the great institutions of mankind, both secular and religious, spring from ritual. Such is the case, as we have seen, with political power, legal institutions, medicine, the theatre, philosophy, and anthropology itself. It could hardly be otherwise, for the working basis of human thought, the process of 'symbolization' is rooted in the surrogate victim. [. . .] [A]ll man's religious, familial, economic, and social institutions grew out of the body of an original victim.[33]

By saying that symbolization is rooted in the surrogate victim, Girard argues that the scapegoat marks the beginnings of an identity regime: as the community consciously defines itself for the first time, in opposition to them.[34] Unbridled mimesis leads the community to become more and more *undifferentiated* – all alike in imitation – until suddenly a scapegoat is marked out as different from everyone else. In a later study of scapegoating, Girard observes how all sorts of distinguishing marks can increase the probability of being singled out as a scapegoat. Ethnic minorities and people with unusual physical characteristics, disabilities or deformities are particularly vulnerable, but also 'there is such a thing as social abnormality; here the average defines the norm. The further one is from normal social status of whatever kind, the greater the risk of persecution.'[35] Both the unusually poor and the unusually wealthy can, Girard observes, be marked out for social abnormality – as, of course, can cultural nonconformists of all kinds.

Just like Zhuangzi with the story of Hundun, and Spinoza with his violent version of the social contract, Girard's theory of scapegoating explains how the need for identity is reinforced by the threat of collective violence. To stand out from the crowd – to fail to adopt an approved identity – is to risk becoming its scapegoat; as Girard puts it, 'An outsider will never be acceptable unless and until his imitation becomes perfect.'[36] Thus, as we saw with Zhuangzi and Spinoza, identity is both the cause and the effect of the threat of violence. Our hunger for identity leads us to emulation, emulation leads to rivalry, rivalry leads to generalized conflict, generalized conflict leads to convergent hostility on a persecuted minority, and persecution leads to the first *social* identity: the communal identity defined by the exclusion of the persecuted.

Things Hidden

The study of mimesis and scapegoating would occupy Girard for the rest of his life. But it is also important to acknowledge that his fundamental motivation was religious. Girard saw himself as a Christian thinker, having converted in 1958–9 while writing the conclusion to *Deceit, Desire, and the Novel.* His conversion was, he always insisted, precipitated by his research into the nature of human desire and violence.[37] But he also quoted with approval the French philosopher Simone Weil's claim that Christianity is an anthropology before it is a theology.[38]

His third major work, *Things Hidden Since the Foundation of the World* (the title is a reference to the Gospel of Matthew [13:35]), published in 1978, was a series of interviews with the French psychiatrists Jean-Michel Oughourlian and Guy Lefort. In it, Girard explains how, in his view, the Judeo-Christian Bible reveals the scapegoat mechanism and the true nature of desire. It is only because of this revelation, Girard proposed, that 'today we are capable of breaking down and analysing cultural mechanisms'.[39] Without it, we would be trapped in the romantic lie. Like Spinoza, Girard reads the story of the Fall of humanity in terms of emulation, or mimetic desire.[40] The Christian gospels, meanwhile, tell the same story that countless myths tell, of a single victim sacrificed to save the community. There is a fundamental difference: the gospels are told *from the victim's point of view*, revealing Jesus to be purely innocent, and the community guilty of mimetic desire. Once this is exposed, Girard believes, the scapegoat mechanism loses its force: a murder cannot expel rivalrous feelings when the community knows that the victim had no part, or only a very small part, in causing them.

This makes the Christian revelation both profound and disturbing for Girard – a complete transformation of human history. By undermining the institution of ritual sacrifice, it leaves humanity without its traditional protection against the destructive power of mimetic desire. And, since Girard sees sacrifice as the foundation of all social and political institutions, the Christian revelation threatens to topple all of them, leaving nothing but mimesis to govern our desires and actions. No wonder Girard would later say: 'I am convinced that history has meaning, and that its meaning is terrifying.'[41] The model of Jesus, however, provides a means of escape from this dire situation, as we will see in Chapter 9.

These three ideas – mimetic desire, the scapegoat mechanism and the Christian revelation which exposes the romantic lie – define Girard's overall philosophy, although part of his genius lies in how he applied his theory to an astonishing range of human stories. But ultimately, what gives rise to the mortal conflicts Girard analysed and foresaw is our original hunger for identity. Summarizing his position in a short 1986 essay, 'Conflict', he put it thus:

> Even the most passionate among us never feel they truly are the persons they want to be. To them, the most wonderful being, the only semi-god, is always *someone else* whom they emulate and from whom they borrow their desires, thus ensuring for themselves lives of perpetual strife and rivalry with those they simultaneously hate and admire.[42]

All our troubles begin from *having* 'persons we want to be'. Our idea of who these persons are will always come from external models, and this will always lead us into perpetual dissatisfaction, rivalry and inner contradiction.

Anti-Existentialism

Sartre's message resonated with a postwar world because it suggested an exciting though daunting prospect: from now on humans must take full responsibility for what they become. Neither religion, nor nationality, nor political institutions, nor even tradition, should ever be taken to answer the fundamental question of who we are. We must instead forge a new path of radical freedom, with nothing from the past to guide us.

Girard, however, ascribes Sartre's existentialist radical freedom to a powerful illusion: the romantic lie of spontaneous individual self-creation. For Girard, there is no possibility of throwing off all imitative models and creating ourselves anew. We will always have models to follow, and the sooner we accept this, the sooner we can identify and address the source of conflict, once and for all.

At times it can appear that even the existentialists were aware that their celebrated radical freedom was an illusion. An interesting example can be found in Beauvoir's 1947 book, *The Ethics of Ambiguity*, which was based on a lecture she gave in 1945.[43]

Beauvoir begins from the strongly existentialist position that humans are, or as she puts it 'man' is, initially driven by a passion that *wills itself.* This 'passion is not inflicted upon him [man] from without', rather 'he chooses it', and in fact 'it is his very being'.[44] Since man has no innate characteristics, his choice cannot be determined by anything internal to him, any more than it is inflicted from without. Thus, this choice '*has* no reason to will itself' at all. Beauvoir explains that 'this does not mean that [the passion] cannot justify itself, that it cannot *give itself* reasons for being that it does not *have*'. Once the passion is there, in other words, it can drive us to choose values and beliefs, which we can then use to justify it after the fact. But first the original passion must emerge spontaneously out of nothing: willing itself into being for no reason at all. Since this passion then drives all the further choices of a free subject, existentialism reduces the whole of human psychology to an event for which there can be no possible explanation: the self-creation of a spontaneous passion from the void.[45]

Later in the text, however, Beauvoir comes close to admitting a different structure, which sounds much more Girardian. By this point she has argued that since humans possess radical freedom they are ethically responsible to acknowledge and affirm this freedom rather than denying it in 'bad faith' – pretending that what they are and do is not really their choice.[46] And yet, she remarks, our freedom is never entirely individual: 'One can reveal the world only on a basis revealed by other men. No project can be defined except by its interference with other projects.'[47] Beauvoir appears to admit here that the self-willing passion that supposedly animates all the original choices of the human subject is not so undetermined and autonomous after all. In fact, it can work 'only on a basis revealed by other men'. There is room, in other words, for Girard's theory, that in fact we can never escape mimesis – that we will always be defining ourselves by comparison with, and emulation of, models.

Girard engages with Beauvoir directly, in an early (1961) review he wrote of her autobiographical work, *Memoirs of a Dutiful Daughter*. Girard's review is called 'Memoirs of a Dutiful Existentialist'.[48] He finds that in places Beauvoir 'succumbs [. . .] to the old myth of romantic spontaneity': the romantic lie that we can free ourselves from all models and determine ourselves in radical freedom.[49] On the other hand, however, he notices that Beauvoir admits to encouraging others, not to spontaneously invent themselves but rather to follow her example. In one instance, he quips that: 'She taught her friend true spontaneity, and he became so well trained that he automatically exclaimed *'C'est de l'opéra'* whenever confronted by a figurative painting.'[50] Girard is teasing here, making explicit how Beauvoir seems to identify 'true spontaneity' with being trained to express the *correct* tastes and opinions on art. In her heart, Girard implies, Beauvoir recognizes subconsciously that *there is no radical existentialist freedom*, that humans are always caught up in imitation of some model that has captivated them, often without realizing it. Before every choice is a guide.

Indeed, Beauvoir must have been aware of how many young people were becoming existentialists, not to honour their radical freedom but because they were captivated by trendy models. The preponderance of existentialist fashions belies the movement's mimetic nature. Many existentialists copied the hairstyle of the singer and actress Juliette Gréco. Others dressed in deliberately worn-out, 'shabby chic' clothing. Most famous of all is the black turtleneck jumper, still recognizable as the uniform of the French existentialist.[51] It is significant how those who followed a movement based on individual self-invention were prone to following trends. In the same vein, Girard points out that, at its best, Beauvoir's autobiography 'is a hymn to individual freedom and the life of the intellect', but 'at its worst, it is a *summa* of the French intelligentsia during the *entre-deux guerres* and the Second World War. It is a description of its way of life and a repertoire of opinions and intellectual fads'[52] – in other words, it is a recipe for copying.

Humans simply cannot help but be mimetic. The more individual they think they are, the more mimetic they are being – for instance, academics are 'a vast herd of sheep-like individualists', as Girard once cuttingly put it.[53] This is his response to the existentialists, and at times even they seem to have admitted to this inherent contradiction.

Self-Branding

Girard remained in the United States for the rest of his life. In 1981, he was appointed the Andrew B. Hammond Professor of French Language, Literature, and Civilization at Stanford University. While he worked there, continuing to apply his theory of mimesis and scapegoating to a range of topics – including texts and stories from world religions and the plays of Shakespeare[54] – a culture was developing around him that would soon be propelled to the ends of the Earth by powerful communication technologies. The creators of Facebook, Google and Instagram were all students at Stanford, as was the first outside investor in Facebook, Peter Thiel, who was taught by Girard and reports being profoundly influenced by him.[55] The Silicon Valley hero Steve Jobs – mimetic model to many – gave a commencement address at Stanford that included a hymn to 'your own inner voice, heart, and intuition', which will 'somehow already know what you truly want to become'.[56] This is the *romantic lie* distilled to a slogan.

Girard did not write much about new technology and social media, although the comments he made about consumer society late in life spoke aptly to it. When, in a series of interviews he gave in 1994 with the journalist Michel Treguer, he critiqued 'the rabid tourists that we are, intent on consuming the entire planet so as to boast upon our return of having travelled more than our friends',[57] he may as well have been describing Instagram.

According to Alice Marwick, who closely observed the

culture of Silicon Valley over a period of many years, the Northern Californian tech industry is driven by an obsession with *self-branding*: the strategic creation of a recognizable identity for promotion and sale.[58] In the wake of the postwar identity crisis, it seems that Sartre and Beauvoir's miracle of *spontaneous* self-creation did not occur. Instead, Girard is vindicated: we have seen the birth of the *strategic* creation of identity, which drives not only Silicon Valley but also many other aspects of our lives in the rest of the world. The ambition to create personal brands and compete for the attention economy of the world has spread mimetically even to people born in remote Indian railway towns, as chronicled in Mishra's 2023 novel *Run and Hide*.[59]

Globally, we are told by advertisements, self-help gurus and even political leaders that we should *be the best version of ourselves*. But, just as Girard would predict, the best version of yourself inevitably turns out to be the emulation of somebody else, or rather a mimicry of a highly edited, artificial representation of somebody else. 'Rushing pell-mell in the direction already chosen by their models,' said Girard in his interviews with Treguer, 'the "mimic men" congratulate themselves on their decisive and independent frame of mind.'[60] The existentialist urge to create your own identity brings us more under the spell of models, millions of which now reside permanently in our pockets, one click or swipe away.

Liberation can only come from a model who leads us out of the pursuit of identity altogether – a paragon on the order of Zhuangzi's Hundun or Spinoza's God, who exemplifies the characteristic of not being anything in particular.

8.
Desiring Otherwise

Saint Augustine and the Pears

'Three quarters of what I say is in Saint Augustine,' Girard said in one interview.[1] To understand Girard's view of the human predicament, we can look at the *Confessions* of this fourth–fifth-century saint. One story that Augustine tells of his youth, with much contrition, is about how he and his friends stole some pears:

> Close to our vineyard there was a pear tree laden with fruit. This fruit was not enticing, either in appearance or in flavour. We nasty lads went there to shake down the fruit and carry it off at dead of night, after prolonging our games out of doors until that late hour according to our abominable custom. We took enormous quantities, not to feast on ourselves but perhaps to throw to the pigs; we did eat a few, but that was not our motive: we derived pleasure from the deed simply because it was forbidden.[2]

At first it seems odd for Augustine to make so much of what seems like a minor teenage prank. But the imagery – the fruit that is enticing simply because it is forbidden – makes it clear that Augustine is using this episode as an allegory for the Fall of humanity.[3]

What Augustine wants to do with this story is probe into the mystery of our fallen condition. He is troubled by the fact that 'there was no motive for my malice except malice'; his petty crime 'lacked even the sham, shadowy beauty with which even vice allures us'.[4] The object was not to eat the pears, nor to upset the owner of the vineyard, nor even entertainment – the theft was not challenging enough to constitute an exciting heist. It was simply to demonstrate his ability to act however he willed. Responding to no reasons, done to no conceivable purpose, this wanton act was meant to express his radical freedom. To conjure an action out of nothing, for no reason at all – what could be more radically free?

However, as Augustine looks back on the act, he realizes that it was not as creative as he thought. In two ways, it was imitative, not original. First, his urge to express his own radical freedom was less a *self*-expression than an imitation of God's omnipotence: 'a crippled sort of freedom, attempting a shady parody of omnipotence by getting away with something forbidden'.[5] Secondly, he engaged in the act only because his friends did it too: 'as I recall my state of mind at the time, I would not have done it alone; I most certainly would not have done it alone.'[6] Augustine struggles to work out the reason for this. It is not simply that he did it for the sake of camaraderie. Nor was it only to share a joke. It was simply that 'to do it alone would have aroused no desire whatever in me, nor would I have done it'.[7]

The theory of mimetic desire is very close to the surface of what Augustine writes here. His desire to act was prompted, or at least enhanced, by the apparent desire of his friends. Yet they were in the same position – only wanting to do it because the others did. This might look like a circular explanation, but in fact it shows how desire can emerge from *nearly* nothing, creating the illusion of the spontaneous will. We are prone to desire what others around us *appear* to desire, and this appearance can be a matter of a misread signal, a rumour, an accident mistaken for a ploy.[8] Once an imitator has taken on a desire from the apparent desire of a model, however, she immediately becomes a model to others, and the mimetic cycle begins. Desire really does emerge where there was none before. It is never conceived by a radically free subject from nothing. Instead, it can emerge from a mimetic cascade, seeded by misperception.

Augustine's story brings out two crucial aspects of Girard's theory of identity. The first is that we readily believe ourselves to be little centres of omnipotence: freely deciding what to do, breaking rules, overcoming constraints and resisting impulses. The second is that the more we entertain this myth, the more profoundly we are in fact influenced by the examples of others. The radical egoist is an avid imitator in denial. This combination of prideful egoism and unconscious mimesis is the formula for the fallen condition in Augustine, and in Girard.

Metaphysical to Mimetic Desire

Girard's theory of mimetic desire is often misunderstood. The most common misunderstanding comes from focusing entirely on the mimetic aspect and overlooking the *metaphysical*. It is, as we have seen, a theory of *identity* before it is a theory of *imitation*: we imitate the desires of others because we seek to *be* them – to possess their identity.[9]

A critical essay by Girard's colleague at Stanford University, Joshua Landy, is a prime example of how this point can be missed. Landy presents Girard's theory as: 'we never want something because it is objectively valuable, or even because it meets our own subjective needs, but only because someone else wanted it before us.'[10] Landy has a very easy time showing such a theory to be implausible and vulnerable to counter-examples. But it is not Girard's theory. Girard does not claim that humans are mere ciphers, mechanically repeating the desires of others. Rather, humans in his view are led towards models by their fundamental desire for *being*. We fall under the influence of a model, Girard tells us, 'who is apparently already endowed with superior being'; we desire the object that the model desires because 'the object must surely be capable of conferring an even greater plenitude of being'.[11]

A model 'apparently already endowed with superior being' means a model who appears to have achieved a definite identity. As Girard never tires of pointing out, the actual objects of desire are of only secondary significance: 'The object is only a means of reaching the mediator. The desire is aimed at the mediator's *being*.'[12] What we ultimately seek is to *be like* our model/mediator. Imitating her desires for specific objects is just a means to achieving her identity. Girard notes how, often, in the novels of Stendhal and Proust, an object loses its desirability once it is possessed, since '[t]he subject discovers that possession of the object has not changed his being'.[13] This shows that it was a *type of being*, not the object, that the subject really wanted.

If we avoid Landy's misinterpretation, we can see that Girard's theory should not lead us to expect the mechanical repetition of desires: on his theory, we seek to emulate, not the specific desires of our model as such but the model's *identity*, which desires can be taken to express. If I want to be like James Bond, for example, I will not necessarily order vodka martinis, shaken not stirred. Emulating Bond could mean coming up with my *own* trademark drink – being, like him, a man who knows what he wants (this is why the product placement in Bond films is of only limited value). The imitation is perfectly visible, but it does not manifest as a crude repetition of a desire for a given object. If you buy a car, you buy *this specific car*. But you also buy *a car of this make and model*, and *a car of this make*, or perhaps *some sort of luxury car*, or *an expensive status symbol*, or even just *an object of this colour*. If I want to emulate your acquisition, what this involves will depend on what description I am taking it under. If I see the object of your desire as *this specific car*, I will want to take the car from you. If I see the object as *a status symbol*, I will want to acquire an equivalent status symbol of my own. Since I am ultimately emulating your identity rather than your purchases as such, how I conceive of the purchase will depend on how I take it to express what I think you essentially are. In buying the car, are you showing yourself to be the type of person who buys a Mercedes, or somebody who likes expensive things, or somebody who likes quality engineering? Imitation will mean very different things depending on the answer, and the answer will depend on what I observe of you and what assumptions I have learned to bring to what I observe.

The same point can help us to see through one of Landy's more strained counterexamples:

> 'Nothing is more mimetic,' declares Girard, 'than the desire of a child.' One wonders, has he ever met a child? Has he ever tried to feed one a brussels sprout? 'Yum yum,' we say, absurdly hoping that our desire for healthy food will carry over mimetically. 'Blech,' says the child, unceremoniously spitting it out.[14]

This counterexample is hardly a case of mimetic desire, since the desire we signal here is for *the child to eat the sprout*, not for *the sprout*. People who desire food eat it. People who desire that *others* eat it push it towards them while theatrically and nonsensically exclaiming 'yum yum'. Children are not stupid. And it is easy to see how a child spitting out the sprout is imitating us at a deeper level, even if we do not spit out sprouts. The *being* we represent to the child, which the child palpably lacks, exudes power, control and autonomy. The best the child can do to emulate this is to exercise what little power they have: the power to refuse. Once we see mimetic desire in Girard's terms – as the emulation of *being* first and foremost – it becomes clear what trap we are caught in. The harder we try to feed the child, the harder the child will resist. The child is emulating the image of power we project.

Landy presents Girard as arguing that 'we never want something because it is objectively valuable, or even because it meets our own subjective needs'.[15] Again, Girard simply does not argue this. He writes of mimetic desire as arising in a subject '[o]nce his basic needs are satisfied (indeed, sometimes even before)',[16] thus implying the existence of basic needs prior to mimesis, and, if we like, of 'objectively valuable' things in the sense of those things that satisfy our basic needs. Regarding desire beyond these basic needs, however, Landy is right in identifying two obvious alternatives to Girard's theory of desire. Perhaps we desire objects, not because our model desires them, but because they are 'objectively valuable' or they meet 'our own subjective needs'.[17] The idea that desire arises from the value of the object is what we can call the *objectivist* theory. The idea that desire arises from needs innate to the subject we can call the *subjectivist* theory.

Girard does not explicitly refute these theories, although he regularly explains how they can arise as illusions from the condition of mimetic desire. Looking at his lifetime, we can see why he does not refute these ideas. As we saw, Girard came of age in the philosophical context of existentialism, which starts from an axiom that denies objective values and any innate human essence. Girard did not need to deal with alternatives that, in his context, had already been rejected by the most prominent philosophers. But *could* he have dealt with them?

Alternative Theories of Desire

To answer this, first ask: why do we crave identity? Why do we find it lacking in ourselves and present in others? The Girardian answer is that we do not have a definite innate self, discoverable by introspection. This effectively rules out the *subjectivist* theory. How can I innately know what my *subjective needs* are without knowing *who I am, as a subject*? I might feel various impulses, which I can follow or resist. But are these my *true* desires or impulses I should overcome if I want to be my true self? I cannot answer without knowing who or what I truly am. For Girard, we all suffer from the condition of the romantic hero profiled in *Deceit, Desire, and the Novel*, who 'cannot draw his desires from his own resources' and 'must borrow them from others'.[18]

What about the objectivist theory? This is sometimes ascribed to Aristotle; it is the theory that the objective goodness or desirability in the object causes us to desire it.[19] In that case, the absence of an innate identity for the subject does not matter: *the objects themselves* can tell the subject what to desire by being good – or at least seeming so.[20] But what does it mean for an object to be good? We could understand this in the way Spinoza does in *Ethics*:

> By 'good', in what follows, I will understand what we certainly know to be a means to conform more and more to an exemplar of human nature that we propose. And by 'bad' I will understand that which we certainly know to impede us in matching to that exemplar. (E 4.Preface)

But in this case, the objectivist theory comes to the same point as the theory of mimetic desire: we want, as good, whatever serves us in emulating an exemplar. Of course, we could design many other theories about how to judge the goodness or objective value of things, and then rationally come to desire them. We might, for instance, make value judgements by consulting our conscience, or reading Scripture, or weighing up consequences, or rationally deducing some natural moral law.

If, however, there is some reason to believe that our value judgements, however we might understand them, are in fact part of a process of identity formation, then we are pushed back in the direction of the theory of mimetic desire.[21] In Chapter 3, I cited some evidence for this belief.[22] I know that people do not like to hear the suggestion that their value judgements are part of their identity-crafting. It makes our strong moral stances seem uncomfortably close to donning a t-shirt emblazoned with the logo of a favourite band or sports team. But it might just be the way things are.

If the objectivist theory holds that we desire things because we judge them to be objectively valuable, and if we make our value judgements as part of a process of identity-crafting, then the objectivist theory is just part of the theory of metaphysical desire. We want things because we want to *be the sort of person* who wants them (actually *getting* things is often much less important than signalling desire or approval – or, often more relevantly, contempt and disapproval). And if, in addition, we lack an innate, introspectable identity – if we have to learn identity from others – then this valuation, tied up with identity-crafting, becomes part of the dynamic of mimetic desire.

Men Become Gods

Girard has some justification, then, in starting from the same point as the existentialists. We are devoid of any innate, definite identity. The problem is not that we have *too little* identity but rather that we have *too much*. We are replete with characteristics and fall into myriad overlapping categories. But which are essential? Which are accidental? Which are intrinsic traits? Which are fleeting states? When, in *Through the Looking Glass*, Alice asks Humpty Dumpty whether words can really mean anything he likes, he replies: 'The question is [. . .] which is to be master – that's all.'[23] So it is with our jagged bundle of personal qualities. In themselves, they can mean anything; the question is, which is to be master? We contain no answer to *that* question. As Girard puts it in a speech he gave late in life on 'Belonging': 'Our own identity is merely the intersection of all that makes us identical to countless others.'[24] What he means is that we have all manner of qualities and characteristics by which we can be identified and grouped with others – we can all belong to any number of crossing and overlapping categories. But the fact that none of these is marked out as decisive – that there is no final, objective answer to the question of which of them ultimately defines us – leaves us with a certain emptiness when it comes to identity.

This is the point from which Girard begins. The subject, as

he describes it, so feels 'the emptiness mentioned in Ecclesiastes growing inside him that he takes refuge in shallow behavior and imitation'. And then: 'Because he cannot face his nothingness he throws himself on Another who seems to be spared the curse.'[25] Now we have to ask why 'Another' seems to be spared the curse of nothingness. This story is often missed in Girard, but it is crucial.

We have seen that any theory of the Fall involves a yearning for a lost, more perfect state. The lost state might be a mere illusion, but, as long as the human soul longs for it, no worldly things can be fully satisfying. Girard finds a vision of the yearned-for state in Dostoevsky, where it appears as 'the promise of metaphysical autonomy'.[26] He goes on:

> For two or three centuries this has been the underlying principle of every 'new' Western doctrine: God is dead, man must take his place. Pride has always been a temptation but in modern times it has become irresistible because it is organized and amplified in an unheard-of way. The modern 'glad tidings' are heard by everyone. The more deeply it is engraved in our hearts the more violent is the contrast between this marvelous promise and the brutal disappointment inflicted by experience.[27]

The Sartrean overtones are hard to miss in this passage. Sartre famously writes that 'man is fundamentally the desire to be God'.[28] But 'God' for him stands for a specific sort of metaphysical ambition: 'the ideal of a consciousness that could be the foundation of its own being-in-itself purely by means of its own consciousness of itself'.[29] The desire to be God is the hope for what Girard calls 'metaphysical autonomy': the ability to *choose what to be* and then *make yourself into that*.

We saw in Chapter 1 why this hope is doomed. What Sartre calls the 'for-itself' and what Zhuangzi called *wu* 吾 – the 'unselfing' self that can choose what to be – is never fully identical to what Sartre calls the 'in-itself', or what Zhuangzi called *wo* 我 – the identity in which the *wu* 吾 chooses to clothe itself. You are never ultimately and finally any *wo* 我, because there alongside it is always your *wu* 吾, holding the power to transform that *wo* 我 or replace it with another and thus revealing that it is no more *the real you* than any other *wo* 我 you could have chosen. Thus, Sartre tells us that the elemental human passion is for the ego to be 'its own foundation, the *Ens causa sui* that the religions know as God'. But, Sartre goes on, 'the idea of God is contradictory and we lose ourselves in vain; man is a useless Passion'.[30] To say that God is 'cause of himself' (*causa sui*) is to say that he is able to *create what he is*. But when we try to create ourselves, the job is never finished. There is always the possibility of adding, subtracting or changing, and even the choice to leave things as they are is an active choice – a continuation of the act of creation – and not an accomplished fact. This is why Sartre finds the idea of God – a being that can somehow *complete* the act of self-causation – contradictory (although perhaps it helps to be outside of time).

What Girard observes, however, is that we are surrounded by *apparent* examples of successful self-creation. Other people can appear to us as Sartrean Gods. He discusses this appearance of success in a chapter of *Deceit, Desire, and the Novel* called 'Men Become Gods in the Eyes of Each Other'. The reason others appear as divine to us is that we are initially aware only of our own emptiness. Others appear to have achieved definiteness. Thus: 'Each one believes that he alone is excluded from the divine inheritance and takes pains to hide this misfortune.'[31] The misfortune is that of *not innately being anything distinct* and *not being able to fully make oneself so*. What creates the illusion that others are spared this misfortune? What we see of others is only their *wo* 我 – their apparent identity. But we are conscious of our own *wu* 吾 – our unselfing self that can always abandon identity and choose another. We can feel our own *wu* 吾, but we cannot see anyone else's. To an unreflectively empiricist subject, going on appearances alone, others are examples of successful, completed self-creation. As Girard puts it, 'the subject does not recognize in the Other the void gnawing at himself. He makes of him a monstrous divinity.'[32]

A mystery remains about why the subject is captured by some models in particular – why we fall into the gravity of some and remain impervious to others. Yet, drawing on literary examples, it is not so difficult to think of explanations. What brought Don Quixote to Amadis of Gaul, Julien Sorel to Napoleon, or Emma Bovary to her heroines? No doubt when they chose those models they were already under the influence of more primordial ones. We begin as children being fed by adults, who appear to possess a sort of completeness of being entirely lacking in ourselves.[33] Among the choices modelled for us by our primordial exemplars are choices of *new* exemplars. Thus (as we saw Quentin Crisp observing in Chapter 5), teenagers escape the influence of their parents by succumbing to the influence of their peers. As Girard puts it: 'The only culture really ours is not that into which we are born; it is the culture whose models we imitate at the age when our power of mimetic assimilation is the greatest.'[34] This is the age when we are most susceptible to the illusion that *ordinary people are distinct; I alone am undifferentiated*. It is the tipping point of the Fall.

The Underground

Girard sometimes refers to the fallen condition as 'the underground', in reference to Dostoevsky's short novel *Notes from Underground*. In *Deceit, Desire, and the Novel* and a full study of Dostoevsky, *Resurrection from the Underground*, Girard argues that this work has been badly misunderstood.[35] Existentialism, he notes, has 'made the word "freedom" fashionable',[36] and Dostoevsky's infamous main character (he is given no name and commonly referred to as 'the underground man') is taken to exemplify spontaneous, existentialist freedom. According to Girard, this represents only how the underground man thinks of himself. His actual behaviour, even as recounted by himself, is pure mimesis.

The novel is in two parts. The first is something like the manifesto of the underground man. The second recounts events from his life. In the manifesto, the underground man proposes that the ultimate aim of human life is to express radical freedom: 'a man, always and everywhere, likes to act as he chooses, and not at all according to the dictates of reason and self-interest'.[37] Even if you shower a man 'with all earthly blessings' and 'give him such economic prosperity that he will have nothing left to do but sleep, eat gingerbread, and worry about the continuance of world history', he will act in some unmotivated, irrational way simply to assert his autonomy: 'He will jeopardize his very gingerbread and deliberately will the most pernicious rubbish, the most uneconomic nonsense, simply and solely in order to alloy all this positive rationality with the element of his own pernicious fancy.'[38] The underground man thus proposes that 'the whole business of humanity consists solely in this – that a man should constantly prove to himself that he is a man and not a sprig in a barrel organ!'[39]

Readers have taken the underground man at his word in this manifesto, according to Girard, so that 'scarcely any of the second part, which is the only truly novelistic part, is noticed except the astonishing freedom – i.e. spontaneity – of the underground character'.[40] Readers take the underground man's actions as expressions of absolute spontaneous will, unguided by reason or anything else – pure demonstrations that he is not 'a sprig in a barrel organ'. And perhaps this is how he intends them. Yet he seems spontaneous only if we ignore how mimetic he is. When he passes a tavern and sees a man thrown out the window, he thinks: 'Perhaps I shall get into a fight too [. . .] and be thrown out of the window.'[41] When he enters the tavern, an officer carelessly moves him out of the way to get to the billiard table. The underground man's response to this insult is to compose 'a really beautiful and charming letter' to the officer, demanding an apology and threatening a duel upon refusal. He fantasizes about the officer being impressed by his eloquence and teaming up with him: 'He could protect me with his influential position, and I could develop his better qualities with my culture and . . . well, my ideas, and all sorts of things could happen!'[42]

These fantastical desires are not spontaneous at all. The underground man's desire is mediated by the officer's. Girard notices that in fact the underground man: 'dreams of absorbing and assimilating the mediator's being. [. . .] He wants to become the Other and still be himself.'[43] The underground man is intent on expressing *his own will*, but since this is raised into defiance of reason and self-interest it is reduced to being determined by *nothing at all* internally. But since the will must be determined if it is to will anything at all, this radical freedom – the clearing of a void inside – can only drive the underground man to be intensely determined by *external* exemplars whose being he covets. Striving so hard to be *himself* makes him all the more mimetic.

The underground man's radical egoism is a mask to hide his mimetic nature from us and from himself: 'the proud wish to be accused of egoism and gladly accuse themselves of it in order better to dissimulate the role that the Other plays in their existence'.[44] Dostoevsky's underground and Augustine's Fall both represent the attempt to assert individuality through radical egoism, which in fact drives the subject into mimesis. You cannot create an identity by sheer force of will, except by falling under the influence of models.

Conflict and Contempt

Mimetic desire is prone to conflict, for reasons we have seen in previous chapters. When I want what you want, we are likely to become rivals for some object of our converging desires. If I want to be like you, I will want to be imitated just as I imitate you. But then, contradictorily, I will *not* want the rivals these imitators inevitably become. Meanwhile, insofar as I want to attract emulators, I will end up competing for influence with others who want the same thing.

Girard's theory of scapegoating, discussed in the previous chapter, was initially advanced as an explanation of how early societies were able to manage these potential conflicts. By concentrating their frustrations onto a single common scapegoat, former rivals can put aside their difference and bond together. In one of Girard's favourite examples, the Roman governor Pontius Pilate and the Jewish king Herod, who had formerly been enemies, became friends through the execution of Jesus.[45] While acknowledging that scapegoating is still a very real phenomenon, Girard holds that our awareness of it has greatly reduced its power in the modern world.[46] A more typically modern way of dealing with mimetic conflict is through mass production. Having more goods reduces the probability that desires will converge on them. Consumer society thus provides a modern means of defusing mimetic rivalry: as Girard says, 'By making the same objects, the same commodities available to everybody, modern society has reduced the opportunity for conflict and rivalry.'[47] But Girard warns that this solution comes with a side-effect. The more mass-produced the objects are, the less satisfying they are to mimetic desire, 'the consequence of which is that one now has an array of objects which go directly from the shop to the bin, with hardly a stop in between'.[48] Things that are easy to acquire, the mass-produced goods of consumer society, lose their value precisely in proportion to the ease of acquiring them. The truly coveted goods are the ones that are hard to get, conferring exclusivity of being upon their possessors.

The issue becomes clear only when we recognize that desire is fundamentally metaphysical: a desire for *identity*. Any scarcity of resources can cause conflict, but agents can weigh up the risk of conflict against the chance of a greater share. Throughout the animal kingdom it is normal for a potential rival to decide that putting up with a meagre portion is better than risking a fight. But humans are subject to mimetic desire, which can bestow what Girard calls a 'metaphysical' significance onto an object guarded by a rival. If the model bars access to an object, it appears to the imitator that the object must be what makes the difference between 'the self-sufficiency of the model and the imitator's lack of sufficiency, the model's fullness of being and the imitator's nothingness'.[49] Thus the choice is not, from the imitator's point of view, between a meagre and a large portion; it is between *nothingness* and *fullness of being*. Any risk of conflict is worth taking on for those stakes. Humans will fight even over *prestige*, which 'is literally fighting over nothing'.[50] A man who disrespects me threatens my identity as *a man not to be trifled with*.[51] To reclaim it, I will risk violent conflict. I will risk my body, my life, time I might spend with my loved ones to gain . . . what? The mere words of a grudging apology? The imaginary substance called *prestige*? No – my identity, which is what mimetic desire is always fundamentally about.

As for consumer society, the confronting implication of Girard's theory is that, however much we might scapegoat manipulative advertising, materialist values, the capitalist system, and so on, the inflation of increasingly unvalued objects is much more directly the result of allowing human desires to proliferate freely. The illusion is no different in this case than in the case of conflict. Whether we overpower our rival or avoid conflict by duplicating her object, we find that getting her out of the way of our object has also drained it of all its desirability. We were not really after the object. We were after *her being*. This being itself is illusory, as we have seen: nobody else's identity is really any more definitive and decisive than our own. And the objects that came to represent this identity to us, which we guessed were the secrets that *made our rival who she was*, turn out not to be what we wanted at all.

Again, this is a psychologically unwelcome theory. We are strongly geared to believe that our dissatisfaction in the world is not caused by our desires themselves. It must, rather, be some oppressive external force, which distorts or represses our desires, or stands in the way of their free expression.

But Girard's theory is that our desires were *already* distorted, repressed and obstructed when they came into existence: the very thing that called them into being is what stands in the way of their satisfaction, and if it stops standing in their way then desire fades. Thus, he warns that the more people 'embrace ideologies of liberation – the more they will in fact be working to reinforce the competitive world that is stifling them'.[52] Ideologies of liberation proliferate the thing they promise to liberate us from. True liberation can only come through escaping the metaphysical yearning that gives rise to desire in the first place.

9.
Salvation and the Imitation of Jesus

Freedom and Mimesis

Girard is not a critic of mimesis as such. Quite otherwise, he holds that: 'Mimetic desire is what makes us human, what makes possible for us the breakout from routinely animalistic appetites, and constructs our own, albeit inevitably unstable, identities.'[1] The problems emerge from our *unawareness* of mimesis. What makes our state a hopeless one is our attachment to the romantic lie that our desires reflect either some order of value inscribed into objects themselves or something *inside* of us, whether an inbuilt identity or a spontaneous act of pure will.

One of the most pernicious illusions identified by Girard is the feeling that freedom could come from liberating our desires from obstacles and external influences. It is these obstacles and influences that generate our desires in the first place. Without them, Girard proposes, we would not be free but enslaved to inflexible appetites:

> If our desires were not mimetic, they would be forever fixed on predetermined objects; they would be a particular form of instinct. Human beings could no more change their desire than cows their appetite for grass. Without mimetic desire

> there would be neither freedom nor humanity. Mimetic desire is intrinsically good.[2]

Sartre, Beauvoir and the underground man could all raise a protest here. If our desires were not mimetic, they might argue, this would not have to condemn us to mere mechanical appetite. Rather, the *radically free ego* could *choose* what to desire. But there is something paradoxical in the notion of choosing without any prompting from appetite, instinct, desire (since that is what is *being* decided) or any external source. Girard feels no need to countenance that possibility.

He does, however, retain the notion that desire is, *in a certain sense*, radically free. He writes:

> Humankind is that creature who lost a part of its animal instinct in order to gain access to 'desire', as it is called. Once their natural needs are satisfied, humans desire intensely, but they don't know exactly what they desire, for no instinct guides them. We do not each have our own desire, one really our own. The essence of desire is to have no essential goal. Truly to desire, we must have recourse to people about us; we have to borrow their desires.[3]

This shows what is wrong with the idea of liberating desire from external influences. It is in fact external influences – mimetic models – that *free* desire, allowing it to break out of the closed tracks of appetite and instinct. The problem is how easily these models can become a newly oppressive force in their own right. Models become rivals as soon as we imitate their desire for a non-shareable object – even if the object is something as intangible as *prestige*. The more a model tries to retain an object, the more driven we will be to take it, intensifying the rivalry towards a crisis point. And all the while, we will be seeking to imitate our models by becoming models ourselves, expanding and multiplying rivalries throughout our social network.

Keeping all this in mind can preserve us from some of the corruptions and misunderstandings of Girard's thought going around. Peter Thiel, for example, draws upon a supposedly Girardian framework to justify his praise of corporate monopolies. In his book, *Zero to One: Notes on Startups or How to Build the Future*, Thiel presents competition in business as a type of mimetic rivalry that stifles innovation: 'Rivalry causes us to overemphasize old opportunities and slavishly copy what has worked in the past.'[4] True innovation, according to Thiel, must come from monopolies that escape petty competition. Girard would be too humble to presume to teach a billionaire technology investor about innovation. But since Thiel claims to be basing his ideas on Girard's theory, we have the right to ask on his behalf: since mimesis is the *source* of both freedom and innovation, how is a business supposed to achieve these by *escaping* mimesis? Girard's expressed view is that: 'In economic life, imitation and innovation are not only compatible but almost inseparable.'[5] Where we do find the successful, innovative monopolies described by Thiel, Girard's theory should lead us to search for their mimetic models, or those of their creators. Thiel must be aware of this at some level, of course, since while presenting the advice to avoid imitation he simultaneously offers himself as a mimetic model: his book is a self-help guide for other startup entrepreneurs. As a political figure, he operates as a model of a more worrying sort.[6]

This case illustrates Girard's maxim that 'individualism is a formidable lie'.[7] Accepting the outward form of Girard's theory, Thiel is unable to abandon the romantic fantasy of a self-directed, creative individual: the entrepreneur, who escapes mimesis and forges an original path. But Girard's theory holds that any attempt at individual liberation from mimesis will only lead into other forms of mimesis and other rivalries. This is why he claims that 'ideologies of liberation' in fact reinforce what they seek to escape.[8] Vulnerable to the formidable lie of individualism, we come to believe that all we need to do is overthrow the laws, rules, prohibitions and structures of power. Then we will suddenly be free to follow our own desires. But *we do not have our own desires*. Those institutions, while undeniably repressive, emerge to manage our imitation of each other, not to suppress our individual wills.

Putting the point in terms of identity makes it starker. If desire is metaphysical, then the structures and regimes that repress desire are really preventing individuals from realizing and expressing their aspirational identities. Liberation movements generally pursue self-determination at some level – for the individual, for an oppressed group, for a nation, etc. And self-determination ultimately means the power to determine your own identity. Yet identity itself remains the greatest instrument of social control that humanity has ever evolved.

Pursuing identity means falling under the influence of models, which causes the formation of cultures and subcultures, preserving group cohesion until the internal tendency towards rivalry causes an implosion. It also means (though we like to hide this from ourselves) seeking the approval, confirmation and emulation of others. Since we cannot know from the inside what our essential identity is, we are intimately dependent on external cues to buoy up our confidence in the path we have chosen. This means that we take on much of the work of policing our visible behaviour for conformity to accepted norms and approved fashions. We hide this from ourselves also, by focusing on the groups and structures we rebel against and studiously turning our eyes from the rebel factions whose approval we sycophantically and meticulously chase. But a useful theory of liberation must take us as we are. Repressive institutions do not stop us from being who we truly are – there is no such thing. Rather, they stop us from imitating each other to maximal intensity.

Desire Can Choose for Itself

Thus far we have concentrated on ideas about individual liberation. But some of Girard's contemporaries proposed a more radical liberation: the liberation, not of the individual desiring subject, but rather of *desire itself*. In 1972 Gilles Deleuze and Félix Guattari published *Anti-Oedipus: Capitalism and Schizophrenia*, perhaps the most radical work to emerge from an academic context in which radicalism was the reserve currency. The book is so avant-garde as to be largely unreadable, but a clear theme is the liberation of desire from the 'Oedipal' system of psychoanalysis. The reference is to Freudian theory, but Deleuze and Guattari clearly see this picture of desire as underpinning our entire sociopolitical system.

'The extensive Oedipal figure,' they write, 'is its displaced represented [*le représenté déplacé*], the lure or fake image, born of repression, that comes to conceal desire.'[9] The Oedipal figure represents desire as a *lack*, and moreover a lack of *specific objects* – originally the mother, or the mother's love, but extending to all the goods that 'normal' subjects are expected to desire. This traps desire into wanting the objects that it is conditioned into wanting, a controlling process on which every stable structure from the nuclear family to the liberal state to the capitalist market is alleged to depend.

Because we see desire as bound to specific objects, Deleuze and Guattari suggest, we are unable to unleash its true power. *True* desire is in fact a boundlessly creative force, always seeking to break the moulds in which it is cast. As Girard paraphrases: 'what resists [the Oedipal figure] is "true" desire, a multivalent and polyvocal force foreign to the demands of representation and imprisonment in structures.'[10] If we will just allow it, desire will flow free of our fixed individual preferences. It will also create new objects to desire. We carve up the world into regions we call 'objects', over which our preferences range, but true desire always tends towards re-homogenizing and then carving up the world in new ways.

We might suspect this far-out agenda as being a relic of a bygone era. But echoes of it can be found in contemporary philosophy. Amia Srinivasan's essay 'The Right to Sex', for example, ends with a stirring passage:

> Desire can take us by surprise, leading us somewhere we hadn't imagined we would ever go, or towards someone we never thought we would lust after, or love. In the very best cases, the cases that perhaps ground our best hope, desire can cut against what politics has chosen for us, and choose for itself.[11]

Arguably, this picture is the unacknowledged background to much radical philosophy, since it holds up an ideal of freedom beyond that of the sovereign individual – the liberal ideal condemned by many leftists as naive and reactionary – and that of empowered *groups* – which risks obscuring authoritarian or oppressive structures within the groups. It celebrates the freedom, neither of the individual nor of the group, but of *desire itself*.

To understand Girard's critique of this notion, it is worth glancing at his comments on Freud's theory of the Oedipus complex.[12] Girard notices that Freud's early theorizing about this complex, in *Group Psychology and the Analysis of the Ego* (1921), makes it look like a special case of mimetic desire. Freud imagines a child identifying with his father: 'The identification is a desire *to be* the model that seeks fulfillment, naturally enough, by means of appropriation; that is, by taking over the things that belong to his father.'[13] Since the mother appears to 'belong' to the father, the child develops a desire for the mother, which is the foundation of the complex. The father appears to block access to the mother, and the child develops an (unconscious) desire to kill the father and possess the mother, hence 'Oedipus'.

Yet by the time of *The Ego and the Id* (1923), Freud has reversed the story. Now the child is *first* said to develop an 'object-cathexis' for the mother and *then*, independently of this, to identify with the father. These independent attachments come into conflict when the child starts to see the father as an obstacle to a *preexisting* desire for the mother. In this text, Girard observes, Freud 'discourages us from thinking that one and the same impulse – the wish to take the father's place *everywhere* – stimulates identification with the model and directs desire towards the mother'.[14] Instead, desire for the mother is taken as simply given.

Girard speculates that Freud abandoned his original mimetic understanding of the complex because it is in tension with the specifically *Oedipal* structure with which he was so taken. Mimetic desire entails that a subject can desire *any* object, so long as it appears to be the key to the model's being. 'The mimetic process detaches desire from any predetermined object, whereas the Oedipus complex fixes desire on the maternal object.'[15] If the child wants to be the father, this can entail a desire for *anything* the child believes to be the key to the father's being; this need not be the mother. When Freud moved away from the mimetic theory, 'he was simply trying to prevent mimesis from subverting his own cherished version of the Oedipus myth'.[16] Girard's theory liberates desire from the structure of that myth. We do not, you might be relieved to learn, have an instinctive desire for our mothers or an instinctive rivalry with our fathers. If such a pattern emerges, it is a special case of a much more general structure: we desire whichever objects seem to bestow being upon our mimetic models, and the models become rivals when they block the way to those objects.

Girard thus expresses many of the same views about desire as Deleuze and Guattari. He too proposes that desire is not inherently trapped into aiming at any specific objects. He too believes that it can, in Srinivasan's words, 'take us by surprise, leading us somewhere we hadn't imagined we would ever go'. He also believes in the power of desire to *create new objects for itself.* Anything at all can become the object of your desire, if you come to believe that it is what bestows upon your model the apparent definiteness of being that you covet. The difference is that Girard does not ascribe to desire any mysterious power of self-generation. He points out that Friedrich Nietzsche, a major influence on Deleuze, 'posits an original and spontaneous desire, a desire *causa sui* called the will to power'. But he asks: 'If desire has no object unique to itself, on what can the will to power be exerted? Unless it is reduced to exercises of mystical gymnastics, it will necessarily pursue objects valorized by others.'[17] Likewise, when Srinivasan speaks of a desire that 'can cut against what politics has chosen for us, and choose for itself', we must ask: how can it choose? Unless we want to imagine desire itself possessing its own little sub-desires to guide its choice, and running into infinite regress, the only possibility is that one subject's desire will follow the signalled desire of *another subject*. When politics does not choose for us, *we choose for each other.*

The Limits of Political Liberation

Girard is not opposed to movements of liberation, but he reminds us that they will always be liberation *to* mimesis. Liberation from instinct, prohibition, law, politics, etc., means freedom to more intensively pursue the being of others. The liberation is genuine, but anyone who feels suddenly freed to 'be themselves' is warned that they will in reality exercise a freedom to *be somebody else*. In cases of what Girard calls 'internal mediation', where you face and interact with your mimetic model,[18] the risk of rivalry and conflict is profound. One by one, your attempts at imitation will fail to bestow upon you the definitive being you believe that you see in your model, until you end up imitating a desire for something that cannot be shared and fall into rivalry.

Even in cases of 'external mediation', where the model is separated from the subject by being distant in space or time, or even fictional, the threat of rivalry is omnipresent. Modelling your identity on an admirable character means being admirable yourself. But the only way to be sure you are admirable is to attract admirers. Mimesis thus leads naturally to ambition, in Spinoza's sense. But the attention of the crowd is a limited resource. Anyone reading your content is for that time *not* reading mine. Even technologies that produce the resource of crowd approval at low cost – e.g. 'likes' on social media posts – do not remove the rivalrous dynamic around it. Making approval cheap does not make the competition for it any less fierce, although it does reduce the satisfaction per unit, as all mass production does.

Girard's advice regarding liberation is therefore to manage expectations. When our desires stop being repressed by power and authority, they are released into an internally generated dynamic that can feel even more oppressive. Failing to understand that the source of oppression is now *their own desires*, people begin to develop conspiracy theories to explain how some invisible force is thwarting them. As Girard puts it:

> At the very moment when the last prohibitions are being forgotten, there are still any number of intellectuals who continue to refer to them as if they were more and more crippling. Alternatively, they replace the myth of the prohibition with one that invokes an omnipresent and omniscient 'power' and can be seen as yet another mythic transposition of the strategies of mimesis.[19]

Unwavering belief that social liberation can solve the deepest riddles of life will only lead us to assign political diagnoses to everything, and to search everywhere for the problem except in our own desires. Girard's conclusion is anti-utopian: 'Whatever political or social system is somehow imposed on them, men will never achieve the happiness and peace of which the revolutionaries dream, nor the bleating harmony which scares the reactionaries.' In the end, people 'will never tire of inventing new forms of conflict'.[20]

For a concrete example, suppose we achieve the communist

dream of abolishing or at least equalizing private property in material goods. This would be well worth doing, if it allowed those in the greatest need to claim a larger share of the world's material resources. At the moment they do not have enough even to satisfy their basic needs, which are in no way mimetic. But we should not fool ourselves into expecting the abolition of private property to end or even really reduce human conflict. There is much more to fight over than the objects we currently value. Fair equality in material goods would just lead to new bases for invidious distinction.[21] The reason is that it was never really material goods we were after, beyond those needed to satisfy basic needs. What we really want is the being that a model appears to possess, and we appear to lack. If we cannot explain the apparent metaphysical gulf between ourselves and the model by a difference in material ownership, then we will find another explanation. My model must have the special being that I lack because of her spouse, her friends, her position on the workers' council, her impeccable proletarian background, the way she commands a crowd. If only I had those things – or, failing that, if only I did not have to live in the shadow of someone who has those things . . .

The Imitation of Jesus

So far Girard appears to have left little room for hope. Liberation from oppression just means deeper entanglement in mimetic desire. Freedom from mimesis, meanwhile, would just mean enslavement to instinct. But Girard's theory does not leave us entirely hopeless. He proposes a way out of the fallen condition, although his thought on this appears to have developed slowly.

In his earliest work, Girard proposes that the way out is simply to renounce the metaphysical desire that leads to mimesis.[22] We imitate others because we seek being, which they seem to possess and have the power to bestow upon us. We can avoid imitation by ceasing the search, but 'this means renouncing pride' – the pride that leads us to think we must be *someone* or *something*.[23] In the novels that Girard takes to be the source of his theory, the hero often achieves a 'conversion' in the end. Girard describes the conversion as follows:

> The hero triumphs in defeat; he triumphs because he is at the end of his resources; for the first time he has to look his despair and his nothingness in the face. But this look which he has dreaded, which is the death of pride, is his salvation. The conclusions of all the novels are reminiscent of an oriental tale in which the hero is clinging by his finger-tips to the edge of a cliff; exhausted, the hero finally lets himself fall into the abyss. He expects to smash against the rocks below but instead he is supported by the air: the law of gravity is annulled.[24]

The hero falls into the 'abyss' of having no identity – looking 'his nothingness in the face'. This is what we fear the most, but when it comes, we feel liberated.

This solution is unsatisfying, however. It remains too attached to the mythology of the *inner void* that we found in the existentialists. When we look honestly within ourselves, what we find is not blank nothingness. It is, on the contrary, a teeming chaos of overlapping half-identities and partial definitions – abundant material for defining an identity, but none of it fully definitive (again, Hundun is wonton). Even if we could clear away all that, as Girard realizes in his later work, this would mean a mere return to instinct and appetite. But he promises much more than this through an experience of sudden self-understanding, 'conversion', which will bring 'a new relationship to others and to oneself'.[25] What kind of relationship this would be is never clarified by the early Girard, although he leaves the hint: 'It is the Other whom one must love *as oneself* if one does not desire to idolize and hate the Other in the depths of the underground.'[26]

In his later work, Girard proposes that the way out lies, not in renouncing imitation, but in imitating the right model: 'There is no solution to mimetism aside from a good model.'[27] Once he revealed his Christian belief to the academic world (and suffered the inevitable loss of credibility among some), Girard could state openly that the right model is Jesus. As we have seen, Girard believes the fundamental importance of the Christian story to lie in its exposure of mimetic desire and the scapegoat mechanism. Christianity, in his view, rejects belief in the mythical power of ritual sacrifice, which in turn is the basis of all human institutions. Modern ideologies that seek to overthrow the church, the state, the family or other social traditions are indebted to Christianity in a way that they cannot understand, so long as they remain subject to the romantic lie that denies the mimetic nature of desire.[28] But in his later writings, Girard also suggests that Jesus serves not only to reveal the innocence of the scapegoat victim (and thus the guilt of the community), he also serves as a different sort of model for us – the only one that can show us how to escape from the destructive mechanisms of mimetic desire.

Girard tells us only a few elusive things about what Jesus signifies as a model. In one book, we find the following crucial passage:

> What Jesus invites us to imitate is his own *desire*, the spirit that directs him toward the goal on which his intention is fixed: to resemble God the Father as much as possible.
>
> The invitation to imitate the desire of Jesus may seem paradoxical, for Jesus does not claim to possess a desire proper, a desire 'of his very own'. Contrary to what we ourselves claim, he does not claim to 'be himself'; he does not flatter himself that he obeys only his own desire. His goal is to become the perfect *image* of God. Therefore he commits all his powers to imitating his Father. In inviting us to imitate him, he invites us to imitate his own imitation.[29]

This is a difficult passage. If we imitate Jesus, who imitates God, are we imitating God? Girard refuses this inference in another book: 'It is not the Father, whom we should imitate, but his Son, who has withdrawn with his Father.'[30] But how do we imitate the Son, Jesus, who 'commits all his powers to imitating his Father', without imitating the Father? Moreover, Girard states that Jesus regards 'the Father and himself as the best model for all humans'.[31] Does this not imply that the Father is, after all, to be imitated (alongside Jesus)?

Another logical problem is that Girard's solution still appears to be attached to a particular religious identity – a Christian one.[32] The desire to pursue Jesus, as one critic, the Korean philosopher Young Woon Ko, puts it, 'may bring about another kind of violence when one's own doctrine and religious tradition is in conflict or becomes exclusive to others'.[33] Is the imitation of Jesus not just the adoption of a religious identity, which, like all identities, will tempt us into conflict when we come into contact with those who do not share it and want to convince us to share theirs instead?

I will not claim to understand all of Girard's obscure

pronouncements on the imitation of Jesus, and the seeming contradictions in his statements might in part arise from his having changed his mind, over the course of a lifetime. I believe that Girard's ideas on identity hold resonance whether we agree with his Christian values or not. And, if one looks closely, there is a coherent thread that connects his metaphysical ideas with the philosophies of Zhuangzi and Spinoza.

God Has No Identity

Suppose we understand God in something like Spinoza's sense: a being with no single identity of its own, instead maintaining a superposition of all possible identities. Imitating this being, as we have seen, means the exact opposite of imitating somebody who appears to have a determinate identity. It means fully embracing the condition of not being anything in particular: flowing among forms and qualities as a many-splendoured, superdeterminate thing, without being defined by any of them.

Girard says very little about how he understands God. The most we get is passages pointing out that God makes his sun rise on the evil and the good and his rain fall on the just and the unjust. 'If we imitate the detached generosity of God, then the trap of mimetic rivalries will never close over us.'[34] If we read this as implying something like the superdeterminate God of Spinoza, then I think we can make some sense out of Girard's notion of the imitation of Jesus. We cannot be very much *like* such a God, since we are finite and limited. We cannot be determined in every possible way, nor can we be expressed as every possible thing. But we *can* imitate God's fundamental characteristic of having no distinct, determinate identity. This, perhaps, is what Jesus achieves in Girard's view, since, as we saw in the mysterious passage above, Jesus 'does not claim to "be himself"'. Rejecting identity, Jesus represents the limited and finite *image* of an infinite and superdeterminate being. This could explain why Girard proposes that we imitate Jesus the Son rather than God the Father directly.

Since this interpretation of Girard's solution trades on depriving Jesus of any distinct identity, it can hardly be called distinctively Christian. Zhuangzi's figure of Hundun (who, like Jesus, is put to a violent death by a community hungry for identity) could equally well model the crucial identitylessness, as could Spinoza's superdeterminate God. But my interpretation does provide some explanation of what Girard means by his occasional suggestions that when we imitate Jesus our relationship with other people becomes one of *identification* rather than imitation. We saw one such suggestion from his early work: 'It is the Other whom one must love *as oneself* if one does not desire to idolize and hate the Other in the depths of the underground.'[35] In his later work we also have pronouncements such as: 'Christ teaches us to look at the other by identifying ourselves with him,'[36] and 'To imitate Christ is to identify with the other, to efface oneself before him.'[37]

Here 'identifying with' the other must mean something other than sharing in a common identity. Girard criticizes shared identity as a goal. For one thing, such sharing is always at risk of descending into a rivalrous competition to be the best or most authentic in exemplifying that shared identity.[38] For another, our own image of a supposedly shared identity will always be that identity *seen from our side*: even if we all agree we have common ground, we each look at this common ground from a different angle. Moreover, as we saw in Chapter 7, communal identity originally arises through the exclusion of the scapegoat, who defines what the community *is* by coming to represent what it is *not*. Thus, Girard concludes: 'If the identity that is immediately noticeable around us is not a source of harmony, it is because it is superficial, false. It has to be replaced with a more real form of identity.'[39]

I propose that this 'more real form of identity' is really *communion in a shared identitylessness*. If I see that you and I are both identityless expressions of superdeterminate being then we are not simply *as one* in a shared identity. We *are* one. There can be no difference in what we essentially are, since each of us is essentially nothing in particular. To use the terms of the *Zhuangzi*, explored in Chapter 2 above, we *merge arcanely* (*ming* 冥) into each other. We join in superdeterminacy. We are Hundun together.

To the criticism that Girard is simply endorsing a religious identity, we can now reply that the imitation of Jesus stands in fact for a sort of open-minded engagement that could support religious pluralism in a much more intimate way than mere tolerance could.[40] If we read Jesus as a being with a limited, determinate identity, then Girard's focus on him only appears to be exclusively attached to the single religious identity of the Christian communion.[41] But if we understand Jesus to stand for superdeterminacy in the way I have proposed, then an integral part of the imitation of Jesus will lead to ecumenical openness and the lack of any exclusive attachment to religious identity. Imitating Jesus will conform to the general practice of merging arcanely into others, once we have escaped from identity, and others will include those with alien religious perspectives. This could just as well be represented by Hundun, or, as Girard suggested in one of his last works, by the figure of Purusha in the ancient Hindu text *Rig Veda* (90). Purusha is ritually sacrificed at the beginning of the world and, like Hundun, is a being without distinct identity ('thousand-eyed, thousand-footed'), who encompasses 'all, that which was and which shall be'.[42]

What does following a superdeterminate, identityless model mean in practice? The English writer and philosopher May Sinclair (1863–1946) (now largely and unjustly forgotten as a philosopher) once proposed that 'a self can only become a perfect self in proportion as it takes on the experiences of other selves; just as it could only become a perfect individual by taking on the experience of millions of other individuals'.[43] Holding onto a single identity means holding onto a single world. If I think I know who I am, then I think I know how the world is also. Things are as I see them, and I cannot see them any other way – nor do I want to, since how I see them is part of who I am. I dig into a single provincial perspective and cannot see things otherwise for fear of losing my being. On the other hand, if I accept the fact of having no determinate identity, then I can flow freely from one perspective to another, following what Zhuangzi calls 'the transformation of things' (*wuhua* 物化). I can take on the experiences of millions of other individuals.

This, I propose, is what Girard means by the imitation of Jesus who imitates God – the Son who 'withdraws' with the Father. In imitating God, Jesus does not pursue a divine identity; he withdraws from the pursuit of identity. By imitating this withdrawal, we enable ourselves to break out of attachment to our own perspective and enter into the perspectives of others. We can truly *identify with* others, in a sense that goes much deeper than the usual one, in which people share a 'common identity' by emulating the same model. Regarding certain comments made by Pope John Paul II on the future of Europe and the world, Girard reflects on the idea 'of an identity of all people'. The Pope, Girard adds, was right to remind us of 'the divine nature of that identity'.[44] The 'divine nature' refers, on my reading, to the core identitylessness or superdeterminacy of God, which is the metaphysical underpinning of the deeper sort of identification I have described. We will not find harmony by combining into some common self. We will not find it in national unity, class solidarity or political alliance, not in the sisterhood of women or the brotherhood of men, not in the united front of the cultural majority or the united resistance of the cultural minority, not in the communion of Christians or Islamic unity or the society of atheist humanists, not in any unity of race or tribe or ideology. We might find many things of value in such common identities, and we might achieve a great deal, but we will only find *harmony* by giving up our attachment to identity in general, by 'vanishing into things'. Only a superdeterminate being can model that for us.

Conclusion: Against Identity

Depend on it, that is the true nature of a spirit – never to be any determinate existence. This is our real immutability – for death can get hold only of that which has a determinate being.[1]

– James Frederick Ferrier

Bondage in all its forms has its stronghold in the inner self and not in the outside world; it is in the dimming of our consciousness, in the narrowing of our perspective, in the wrong valuation of things.[2]

– Rabindranath Tagore

Identity, which is death, is the god of the intellect.[3]

– Miguel de Unamuno

Hundun died when the world gave him a face, and it seems, too, that we will also die from pursuing an identity. We die, firstly, because identity fixes us in place while the world is always transforming. Holding onto identity means failing to keep up with the world and being left behind as time flows on. We also die from identity because it is only things with definite identities that *can* die. Death means being so transformed as to no longer count as your *self* – this can only happen if you have a self to lose. And, in the most extreme case, identity makes it hard for us to live with each other. For you to remain yourself, the world must stay a certain way, but this will never be quite as how others need it to be to remain themselves. Identity cannot be isolated from the dynamics of emulation, rivalry and ambition that give rise to it. It will always lead to conflict. The power of these dynamics means that beings with identities cannot, in the end, share a world peacefully with each other, no matter how much they might wish they could.

This book has delved into the writings of three different thinkers, separated by vast distances of spacetime, to dig out a philosophy of going against identity – of escaping the self. I have tried to trace their beliefs on how we can achieve this escape. I cannot claim to understand it in any practical sense.[4] As I wrote in a previous book, I have not escaped the mire of identity. I too find myself taken by attractive exemplars while simultaneously falling into the romantic illusion that my desires and ambitions have come from myself alone. I too flatter myself that I am motivated by objective truths and transcendental values, which others are too foolish to recognize or wicked to want, rather than suspecting that perhaps I am after glory and status within a certain ideological identity and others are just following a different model. Try as I might to embrace the teaching I have presented here, pride manages to keep sneaking back into the driver's seat of my actions.

But I have caught the glimmer of an escape route in the pages of Zhuangzi, Spinoza and Girard. The first step is to see the trick of identity for what it is: your identity was never yours in the first place. It is always borrowed from a model. We are driven towards models by our most powerful instinct: our hunger for being, our struggle for survival. Being is always being *as something*. Survival is always survival *as something*. As what? That is the question of identity, which pushes us towards models as answers.

Yet as soon as we try to define being for ourselves, it recedes to an infinite distance. Chasing it, we threaten others and exhaust ourselves. Our world has developed a powerful identity regime. Everyone is visible, everyone monitors everyone else, and the social costs of failing to curate and present the right identity can be devastating.[5] Cutting-edge media technologies have combined with deep tendencies that evolved during our species' prehistoric process of self-domestication to pile the pressure on individuals to create and curate identities for themselves and police the identities of others.

Escaping from the trap of the self means finding a different model of living to abide by. If we could embrace a model of *superdeterminacy*, of a type of being that embraces all possible identities while being defined by none of them, then we could achieve a new sort of peace, both inner and outer. We could flow along with things happily, not worrying about mutating from our spuriously definite selves. We could love others, not because they share an identity with us, but because they are different from us, as we indeed, in our Hundun-wonton corelessness, contain difference in ourselves. Instead of being threatened by what we do not understand, we could welcome its power to transform us, knowing that being transformed in a thousand different ways will not take us away from who we are, but will, on the contrary, drive us further into our own multifarious and superdeterminate depths. We could stop fighting against the irresistible currents of a world in which things, despite our sternest ethical injunctions, refuse to simply be what they are – ourselves included. Rather than meeting others in a shared identity – which always carries the risk of opposing us to some excluded third party or becoming an object of rivalry between us – we could merge darkly into identitylessness together. And then, like the fluid face of Hundun, we could always be ready to be transformed into something new, never fixed into a single visage.

If you pursue this path of escape, however, do not expect support from others. Attachment to identities is not simply a matter of individual desire. It is socially reinforced by our self-domesticating tendency. Powerful peer groups form to enforce conformity in the boardroom, the party meeting, the playground and online 'communities'. Diverging from recognized identities involves a *loss of face*, to use an expression made apt by the Hundun story. Anyone who escapes the ordinary categories and distinctions by which we define ourselves and each other indirectly threatens the identities of other people, who are likely to react with a violent impulse to *reenvisage* this defector from the identity regime. By refusing the distinctions of prestige and status, you threaten to reveal their arbitrariness to the world, and those whose very being depends on those distinctions will fight to prevent that, without even knowing what they are doing.

This might be one reason why activism based on stirring up moral feelings, which we have seen to be intimately bound up with our sense of identity, seems to have spawned political factionalism and media wars more than creative solutions to our problems. Our global problems are too big and complex to be reduced to simple morality tales. They do not lend themselves to punitive coalitions and moral pressure groups.[6] Moral feelings become instead a new source of competitive games – a way to glory together in a political identity where we compete to best exemplify the right way of doing things, while humiliating and destroying those who threaten that identity, whether from the inside or the outside.

What we really need is innovation: new ways of thinking, being and acting to deal with challenges we did not foresee when we settled into our current forms and habits. Economic theorists from various ideological positions have diagnosed our current problems as deriving, not simply from material and institutional deficiencies, but from a decline in real innovation.[7] For instance, our chance of bringing the whole human population up to a decent standard of living without unacceptable ecological consequences depends on finding new ways to do old things – not just technological innovations, but broader innovations in living.[8] A farmer risks her livelihood by trying out a new pattern of irrigation or crop-rotation. A gas engineer violates company policy to perform a better installation undreamt of in the official manuals. Individuals risk social death by deciding to possess a smaller wardrobe, drive a less ostentatious vehicle, or skip the latest upgrade on their mobile phone. A politician doubts out loud the dogma that the entire purpose of government is to ensure that an already giant economy is 4 per cent larger each year.

But people do not innovate well under the close surveillance of an identity regime. The crowd does not tolerate being snubbed by those who presume to operate without its approval. Maintaining the correctness of its own identity means condemning those who diverge from it. This is why internal critics in a religious or political movement are dealt with much more harshly than the external enemies the movement claims to be united against, or why artistic movements often demean the achievements of their most inventive members. The crowd might believe that it is rooting out threats to its security, but in fact it is looking for threats to its *identity*: a crowd is united by a feeling of having discovered the right way to act and be, and nothing challenges the basis of this collective identity more than the prospect of individuals achieving admirable results by diverging from its norms. In my own university sector, I have long observed that peer review, a system of academic community policing, whose ostensible purpose is to filter out substandard research, functions also to enforce mediocrity. The academic herd is incapable of appreciating alternatives to its entrenched practices, since doing so would be incompatible with its self-conception as a community that has already reached the optimum balance of innovation, excellence and diversity. Understanding our innovation famine requires us to understand how many of our communities, whatever their stated purpose might be, are really identity regimes driven by egotism – patrolled and sustained by individuals determined to persevere in a certain idea of themselves: a fragile idea that cannot bear much novelty.

Some of those who recognize the cultural constraints that our identity regimes place on creativity imagine the solution to lie in a reinvigorated individualism, summed up in Steve Jobs's opposition between 'the noise of others' and 'your own inner voice'.[9] Injunctions to heed your inner voice are not exactly rare in our world, so we must wonder whether this message fails because it is mistaken on a crucial point. According to the philosophy examined here, it is. Individualism falls for the romantic lie. Attempted self-emulation does not lead out of the trap of identity. It drives you deeper into imitation and rivalry while also hiding this truth from yourself. The 'inner voice' is just the noise of others echoing inside your own emptiness. Individual identity is not a way to escape from the crowd; it is the receiver for remote control *by* the crowd, whose power over the individual lies in pride and the fear of shame. A real escape requires a different type of exemplar – really an anti-exemplar, to subvert the whole process of identity-formation and help us to break away from the pursuit of identity altogether.

We have been on a strange journey. I have founded this book on an unusual claim: that thinkers as different as Zhuangzi, Spinoza and Girard share a common core idea. The claim seems outrageous because these thinkers communicated in such different ways. Zhuangzi's texts are a haunted cacophony of myths, dreams and jokes. Spinoza, as a poem by Jorge Luis Borges so perfectly expresses it, 'ground a stubborn crystal' of logical deductions.[10] Girard turned a cold and clinical eye to human behaviour as presented in theatre, literature, mythology and anthropology. But in these wildly different visions, they all saw a pathway leading out of the prison of the self. Zhuangzi writes of losing yourself. Spinoza traces a transition from acquiescence of *self* to acquiescence of *soul* – the latter bringing real peace, where the former brings at best only an anxious and fragile success. Girard speaks of the imitation of Jesus, who does not claim to be himself and stands for the identification with the other to the point of self-effacement.

But we seem to have arrived back where we started. The core claim of Zhuangzi, Spinoza and Girard is that when we seek our *selves* – when we strive for an identity of our own – we end up finding *another*: a model to guide our being. The path that leads away from identity seems to lead to exactly the same place – to the other, with whom we are invited to 'merge arcanely'. The difference is that now we find what we were seeking, rather than the very opposite. If you look for yourself, you will only find another. If you look for others, there they are all around you. When we stop looking for ourselves in others, we will see them as they really are. I believe that we have barely begun to live in the world together. Our drive for identity is always getting in the way. Spinoza's God is sometimes called 'impersonal', but in fact it is more personal than any individual person could be. The image of God is the immeasurable variety of human life – the deep personal stories that lie always beyond our shallow judgements and discriminations. If we are made in the image of God, it is as Hundun, before the face.

When Han Suyin, the identity-defying heroine of *A Many-Splendoured Thing*, says at the end of the novel, 'I have dreamed a wonderful dream', she has given up the search for herself and fully embraced what she calls a many-splendoured thing – a thing that is both her and the world. She has seen the world in the vision of Zhuangzi: a shifting, kaleidoscopic vision in which all things merge into all others and no fixed identities block the flow of transformation – in which, to use another powerful image from Zhuangzi, the wind of heaven blows through the pipes of every creature (Z 2.2–5).

Besides the 'many-splendoured thing', which comes from a Shakespearean sonnet, there is another Shakespearean echo in Suyin – in the passage about dreaming a wonderful dream. It is of Bottom the Weaver in *A Midsummer Night's Dream*, who cries out: 'I have had a most rare vision. I have had a dream past the wit of man to say what dream it was. Man is but an ass if he go about to expound this dream' (IV.i.206–9). The dream was that he *was* an ass – or at least had the head of one, leading his friend the playwright Peter Quince to exclaim: 'Bless thee, Bottom, bless thee. Thou art translated' (III.i.110). Upon awakening, Bottom resolves: 'I will get Peter Quince to write a ballad of this dream. It shall be called "Bottom's Dream" because it hath no bottom' (IV.i.215–17).

Perhaps Zhuangzi, Spinoza and Girard were asses for going

about to expound this dream, but they did try. What they saw is that we are all translated – into each other. When Quince sees Bottom in his changed state, Bottom's first response is to accuse Quince of seeing 'his own ass head'. Bottom is not wrong. The thought of identity makes donkeys of us all. We see ourselves when we look to others, and we find others when we look for ourselves. It is only in the bottomless dream that we see things as they are: we are the others and the others are us, not because we share an identity, but because we are alike in identitylessness – all expressions of a single superdeterminacy – all the uncarved Hundun below the surface of everyone and everything. Bottom's dream is an enchanted forest of translation and misrecognition, where the fairies' magic makes a farce of our proud identifications and shows what fools we mortals be. To restore his feeling of reality, Bottom calls it a dream, but was it? If we lose sight of the enchanted vision, returning in the light of morning to all our discriminating and distinguishing and carving out of identities, what hope can there be for the world?

As we are run ragged, busily defining our identities, the ground shifts under our feet. We define ourselves by our work, then a change in circumstances prevents us from working. We define ourselves by our good looks, then we age. We define ourselves by nationality and then find that nations change their character and mean different things to each new generation. We define ourselves by religion, and then we lose our faith, or our church loses its way (at least as we see it). We define ourselves by our success in business or politics or activism or education, and then find upstarts changing the game, so that where once we were winning now it is not even clear that we are playing. Most of all, we never achieve the secure identity we seek. Identity runs against the grain of the world, which is fundamentally the transformation of things – *wuhua* 物化. Moreover, the conditions of its pursuit are contradictory: others must simultaneously imitate us (to affirm our identity) and not imitate us (so as not to threaten our unique status).

All the same, a world without identity is terrifying. How can we live without knowing who we are, or who others are? Drowning in a world where nothing is certain, where half of what we think we know is probably mistaken and the other half will soon be out of date, fear drives us to cling to the driftwood of various definitions. We strive ever more ferociously to craft, curate, promote and defend definite selves out of the chaos of character, taste, class, nationhood, family and desire we find whirling within. We try to sculpt the tempest all around us into a recognizable story in which we can play a familiar character, to define values against which we can measure up and triumph. When this fails to give us the comfort we expect, we blame others instead of seeing the plain impossibility of our aim. Real wisdom is to find comfort in recognizing that the outer storm and the inner chaos are one and the same. Ultimately, everything is made of translation, yourself included. Drill him all you like, Hundun will always remain, transformed and resurrected the moment he is destroyed. To feel his living presence is to feel a truly universal love for the world, which is universal not because it is all-encompassing but because it is beyond identity. It loves others for what they are, not what we want ourselves to be. Bless us all, we are translated.

We have read Yunkaporta's advice: 'You must allow yourself to be transformed through your interactions with other agents and the knowledge that passes through you from them.'[11] Mishra calls for something similar: 'some truly transformative thinking, about both the self and the world'.[12] You cannot find thinking more transformative than what is provided by the three figures we have studied in this book. They worked in entirely different historical contexts, drawing on different religious and philosophical backgrounds. But they all lived in the wake of a collapsing identity regime. They did not respond, as many others did, by calling for the construction of a new set of identities or launching heroic ideals of individual self-invention. Rather, they responded by arguing passionately and eloquently, in their entirely different styles, against identity.

Acknowledgements

It is impossible to thank everyone who played a crucial role in bringing about this book. All I can do here is name a few names and hope that the many others will know who they are and that I hold them in my heart, if not in my immediate recall at this moment.

Drafts of this book were read, in part or whole, by Christoph Schuringa, Emily Thomas, Wim de Reu, Georg Moeller and Scott Sprenger. I was honoured to be recommended to Penguin by Richard Whatmore, on the advice of Quentin Skinner – both acts of tremendous faith and generosity of spirit. Susan James, my mentor since 2006, remains an unwavering support and source of ideas and inspiration.

I am blessed to work in a wonderful department, full of intellectual energy, kindness and wisdom. I hereby acknowledge my debt of gratitude to all my colleagues and students, who keep me going every day and help me try out my ideas on a sharp but gentle audience. I also thank the University of St Andrews for granting me the time to write and research this book.

My supervisees, past and present, have guided me perhaps more than I have guided them: Antonio Salgado Borge, Deryn Thomas, Xiao Qi, David Harmon, Dario Zoppetti, Megan Gottschall and Aliza Ashraf.

My previous book, from which some of the material for this one was drawn, was similarly supported by my department and university. I also thank James Harris for organizing a symposium on it, where invaluable comments were provided by Eric Schliesser (a steadfast support to me since the earliest days of my research on Spinoza), Hannah Laurens and David Harmon. Helen de Cruz, demonstrating the kindness of strangers, contracted me after reading my book to organize several events, one involving Yarran Hominh, one involving Ian James Kidd, and a written symposium with wonderful responses from Stephen Harrop, Kristin Primus and Brook Ziporyn. The scholarship of all these people has also provided me with a rich reservoir to draw upon.

Writing about Zhuangzi is a very daunting prospect for a non-specialist. I thank Brook Ziporyn, Georg Moeller, Wim de Reu and Paul Napier for their guidance – please do not blame them for the many remaining errors. I am grateful for the scholarship of so many, whose tireless work has made these wonderful texts at least partly accessible to non-sinologists – the sources I have cited give only the tip of the iceberg.

Conversations with Gregory Lee, who founded the Chinese Studies department at St Andrews, helped me to understand the rich and complex relationship between modern China and what came before; he also taught me a bit of 文言文. Nicholas Morrow Williams, my childhood friend, was the first person to tell me to read the *Zhuangzi*, although it took me much too long to take his advice. And he introduced me to the beautiful languages and cultures of East Asia; only my mother preceded him in this.

My friends have sustained me through the writing of this book; many of its words were written under their roofs, developed through their conversation, and, in truth, plagiarized from them in many instances. I hope they can forgive me, and I thank them for enduring hours of ridiculous and rambling thoughts with unfailing good nature. I do not know how anyone could write or think without having a space like this in their life.

The editorial team at Penguin are like nothing else in this world. I have lost track of the number of Penguin employees who have read my book. I am grateful to Penelope Vogler, Violet Zhang and all the others who read and helped to promote it. Claire Péligry and Anna Tuck dealt with my mistakes with precision, patience and grace. Without Casiana Ionita, who took a chance on this weird concept, I doubt it would ever have materialized. Most of all, I cannot adequately thank Hana Teraie-Wood, the best editor an author could hope to have. If you enjoy reading any of the sentences in this book, you most likely have her to thank, and without her unflagging enthusiasm and willingness to enter into another's perspective, the book would not exist at all.

The love of my family breathes through every page I write. Without them I could not have written this book, or anything. The memory of my father drives me to remain permanently curious and to always look beyond the horizon, as he did. My mother's voracious, transcultural, polyglot appetite for knowledge and stories brought me into a vast world of literature from my earliest days; this book marks where I have got to in a journey that I began with her. My sister, my nephew and my extended family – extended in every direction! – remind me that the world is wide and wonderful and teeming with secret blessings, however difficult things might be at any time. They always believe in me and teach me to believe in others.

Lauren, to whom the book is dedicated, makes my life feel like a happy and impossible dream. Although the philosophy in this book comes from Zhuangzi, Spinoza and Girard, rather than from myself, I still worry that it is presumptuous of me to recommend it. Who am I to presume to tell others how to live? Except I *can* say that I have found happiness. But largely I have found it in my wife. And we have talked, every day, about the thoughts in this book for so long that I think of it as a joint creation.

Finally, I thank you, whoever you are, for doing me the honour of reading my book. I hope you find something helpful in it.

Bibliography

Abani, Chris. *The Face: Cartography of the Void*. Brooklyn: Restless Books, 2016.

Alison, James. *The Joy of Being Wrong: Original Sin Through Easter Eyes*. New York: Crossroad, 1998.

Allinson, Robert. 'On the Question of Relativism in the Chuang-Tzu'. *Philosophy East and West* 39, 1 (1989): 13–26.

Anscombe, Gertrude Elizabeth Margaret. 'The First Person'. In *Metaphysics and the Philosophy of Mind: Collected Philosophical Papers: 2*, 21–36. Oxford: Blackwell, 2002.

Appiah, Kwame Anthony. *The Ethics of Identity*. Princeton: Princeton University Press, 2007.

—*The Lies That Bind: Rethinking Identity*. London: Profile Books, 2018.

Aquinas, Thomas. *Summa Theologica*. Rome: Forzani, 1894.

Aristotle. *Complete Works of Aristotle: The Revised Oxford Translation*. Edited by Jonathan Barnes. Princeton: Princeton University Press, 1984.

Attas, Syed Muhammad Naquib al-. 'The Mysticism of Hamzah Fansuri'. PhD, School of Oriental and African Studies, 1966.

Augustine. *Confessions*. Translated by Maria Boulding. New York: New City Press, 1997.

—*Confessions*. Translated by Sarah Ruden. New York: Random House, 2018.

Aw, Tash. *The Face: Strangers on a Pier*. Brooklyn: Restless Books, 2016.

Bailie, Gil. *Violence Unveiled: Humanity at the Crossroads*. New York: PublishDrive, 1996.

Bakewell, Sarah. *At the Existentialist Café*. London: Penguin, 2016.

Baumeister, Roy. *Evil: Inside Human Violence and Cruelty*. New York: Henry Holt and Company, 2015.

—*The Self Explained: Why and How We Become Who We Are*. New York: Guilford Press, 2022.

Baxter, Donald. 'The Discernibility of Identicals'. *Journal of Philosophical Research* 24 (1999): 37–55.

Beauvoir, Simone de. *Memoirs of a Dutiful Daughter*. Translated by James Kirkup. London: Penguin Classics, 2001.

—*The Ethics of Ambiguity*. Translated by Bernard Frechtman. Secaucus: The Citadel Press, 1972.

—*The Second Sex*. Translated by Constance Borde and Sheila Malovany-Chevallier. New York: Vintage Books, 2011.

Billeter, Jean-François. *Leçons sur Tchouang-tseu*. Paris: Allia, 2014.

Boethius. 'Consolation of Philosophy'. In *Theological Tractates / The Consolation of Philosophy*. Translated by H. F. Stewart, E. K. Rand and S. J. Tester. Cambridge: Loeb, 1989.

Bootle, Emily. *This is Not Who I Am: Our Authenticity Obsession*. Croydon: Ortac Press, 2022.

Borges, Jorge Luis. *The Borges Reader*. Edited by Emir R. Monegal. New York: Plume, 1981.

Bourke, Joanna. *The Second World War: A People's History*. Oxford: Oxford University Press, 2001.

Buruma, Ian. *Spinoza: Freedom's Messiah*. New Haven: Yale University Press, 2024.

Butler, Judith. *Giving an Account of Oneself*. New York: Fordham University Press, 2005.

Campanini, Massimo. *An Introduction to Islamic Philosophy*. Translated by Caroline Higgitt. Edinburgh: Edinburgh University Press, 2008.

Cantor, Lea. 'Zhuangzi on "Happy Fish" and the Limits of Human

Knowledge'. *British Journal for the History of Philosophy* 28, 2 (3 March 2020): 216–30.

Carlisle, Clare. *Spinoza's Religion: A New Reading of the Ethics*. Princeton: Princeton University Press, 2021.

Carreyrou, John. *Bad Blood: Secrets and Lies in a Silicon Valley Startup: The Story of Elizabeth Holmes and the Theranos Scandal*. London: Picador, 2023.

Carroll, Lewis. *The Annotated Alice: Alice's Adventures in Wonderland and Through the Looking Glass*. Edited by Martin Gardner. London: Penguin, 2001.

Cayley, David. *The Ideas of René Girard: An Anthropology of Religion and Violence*. Independently Published, 2019.

Chan, Alan. 'Neo-Daoism'. In *The Stanford Encyclopedia of Philosophy*. Edited by Edward N. Zalta, Summer 2019. Stanford: Metaphysics Research Lab, Stanford University, 2019. https://plato.stanford.edu/archives/sum2019/entries/neo-daoism/.

—'The Daode Jing and Its Tradition'. In *Daoism Handbook*. Edited by Livia Kohn, 1–29. Leiden: Brill, 2000.

Chan, Wing-tsit. *A Source Book in Chinese Philosophy*. Princeton: Princeton University Press, 1963.

Chen, Ellen Marie. *In Praise of Nothing: An Exploration of Daoist Fundamental Ontology*. Xlibris Corporation, 2010.

Chen, Guying. *The Philosophy of Life: A New Reading of the Zhuangzi*. Leiden: Brill, 2016.

Chinn, Ewing. 'Zhuangzi and Relativistic Scepticism'. *Asian Philosophy* 7, 3 (1997): 207–20.

Cockshott, Paul. *How the World Works: The Story of Human Labor from Prehistory to the Modern Day*. New York: Monthly Review Press, 2019.

Collingwood, Robin George. *The New Leviathan; Or, Man, Society, Civilization and Barbarism*. Oxford: Oxford University Press, 1942.

Confucius. *The Analects of Confucius*. Translated by D. C. Lau. Harmondsworth: Penguin Books, 1979.

Cowdell, Scott. *René Girard and Secular Modernity: Christ, Culture, and Crisis*. Notre Dame: University of Notre Dame Press, 2015.

Crisp, Quentin. *The Naked Civil Servant: How to Become a Virgin, and Resident Alien*. New York: Quality Paperback Book Club, 2000.

Debray, Eva. 'Imitation des affects et production de l'ordre social'. In *Spinoza et les passions du social*. Edited by Eva Debray, Frédéric Lordon and Kim Sang Ong-Van-Cung, 129–65. Paris: Éditions Amsterdam, 2019.

Deleuze, Gilles, and Félix Guattari. *Anti-Oedipus: Capitalism and Schizophrenia*. Translated by Robert Hurley, Mark Seem and Helen R. Lane. New York: Penguin Classics, 2009.

Derrida, Jacques. *Points . . . : Interviews, 1974–1994*. Stanford: Stanford University Press, 1995.

Descartes, René. *Oeuvres de Descartes*. Edited by Charles Adam and Paul Tannery. Paris: Cerf, 1897.

—*The Philosophical Writings of Descartes*. Translated by John Cottingham, Robert Stoothoff, Dugald Murdoch and Anthony Kenny. Cambridge: Cambridge University Press, 1985.

Diefenbach, Katja. 'Hallucinating Colonialism: Spinoza and the Silence on Colonial Slavery in Early Modern Philosophy'. American University and Collège international de philosophie, Paris, 2016.

Dostoevsky, Fyodor. *Notes from Underground*. Translated by Jessie Coulson. Melbourne: Penguin, 2010.

Douglas, Alexander. 'Spinoza and Social Science'. In *Encyclopedia of Early Modern Philosophy and the Sciences*. Edited by Dana Jalobeanu and Charles T. Wolfe. Springer International Publishing, 2021.

—'Spinoza, Money, and Desire'. *European Journal of Philosophy* 26, 4 (2018): 1209–21.

—'Spinoza's Theophany: The Expression of God's Nature by Particular Things'. *Journal of Early Modern Studies* 11, 2 (2022): 49–69.

—'Spinoza's Unquiet Acquiescentia'. *Proceedings of the Aristotelian Society*, 2020.

—'The Affects'. In *Spinoza*. Edited by Andre Santos Campos, 106–17. Exeter: Imprint Academic, 2016.

—*The Philosophy of Hope: Beatitude in Spinoza*. Oxford: Routledge, 2024.

Dumouchel, Paul. *The Barren Sacrifice: An Essay on Political Violence*. Translated by Mary Baker. East Lansing: Michigan State University Press, 2015.

Dupuy, Jean-Pierre. *Le Sacrifice et l'envie – le libéralisme aux prises avec la justice sociale*. Paris: Calmann-Levy, 1994.

Eddington, Arthur. *Nature of the Physical World*. London: J. M. Dent & Sons, 1942.

Erixon, Fredrik and Björn Weigel. *The Innovation Illusion: How So Little is Created by So Many Working So Hard*. New Haven: Yale University Press, 2017.

Falkenhausen, Lothar von. 'The Economy of Late Pre-Imperial China: Archaeological Perspectives'. In *The Cambridge Economic History of China*. Edited by Debin Ma and Richard von Glahn, 1: 15–51. Cambridge: Cambridge University Press, 2022.

Fanon, Frantz. *The Wretched of the Earth*. Translated by Constance Farrington. New York: Grove Press, 1963.

Feloni, Richard. 'Peter Thiel Explains How an Esoteric Philosophy Book Shaped His Worldview'. *Business Insider*, 11 October 2014. https://uk.finance.yahoo.com/news/peter-thiel-explains-esoteric-philosophy-221708682.html.

Feuer, Lewis. *Spinoza and the Rise of Liberalism*. London: Routledge, 1987.

Garfield, Jay. *Losing Ourselves: Learning to Live without a Self.* Princeton: Princeton University Press, 2022.

Girard, René. *A Theatre of Envy*. Leominster: Gracewing Publishing, 2000.

—*All Desire is a Desire for Being*. Edited by Cynthia Haven. London: Penguin Classics, 2023.

—*Anorexia and Mimetic Desire*. Translated by Mark Anspach. East Lansing: Michigan State University Press, 2013.

—*Battling to the End: Conversations with Benoît Chantre*. Translated by Mary Baker. East Lansing: Michigan State University Press, 2009.

—*Deceit, Desire, and the Novel: Self and Other in Literary Structure*. Baltimore: Johns Hopkins University Press, 1976.

—*Evolution and Conversion: Dialogues on the Origins of Culture*. London: Bloomsbury, 2017.

—*I See Satan Fall Like Lightning*. Leominster: Gracewing Publishing, 2001.

—'Memoirs of a Dutiful Existentialist: Simone de Beauvoir'. In *Mimesis and Theory: Essays on Literature and Criticism, 1953–2005*. Edited by Robert Doran, 50–55. Stanford: Stanford University Press, 2008.

—*Mimesis and Theory: Essays on Literature and Criticism, 1953–2005*. Edited by Robert Doran. Stanford: Stanford University Press, 2011.

—*Resurrection from the Underground: Feodor Dostoevsky*. Translated by James Williams. East Lansing: Michigan State University Press, 2012.

—*Sacrifice*. Translated by Matthew Pattillo and David Dawson. East Lansing: Michigan State University Press, 2011.

—*The Scapegoat*. Translated by Yvonne Freccero. Baltimore: Johns Hopkins University Press, 1989.

—*Things Hidden Since the Foundation of the World*. London: Bloomsbury Academic, 2016.

—*To Double Business Bound: Essays on Literature, Mimesis and Anthropology*. Baltimore: Johns Hopkins University Press, 1988.

—*Violence and the Sacred*. New York: Bloomsbury Academic, 2013.

—*When These Things Begin: Conversations with Michel Treguer*. Translated by Trevor Cribben Merrill. East Lansing: Michigan State University Press, 2014.

Girardot, Norman. *Myth and Meaning in Early Daoism*. Magdalena: University of Hawaii Press, 2009.

Goldstein, Rebecca. *Betraying Spinoza: The Renegade Jew Who Gave Us Modernity*. New York: Knopf Doubleday, 2009.

Graham, Angus. *Disputers of the Tao: Philosophical Argument in Ancient China*. La Salle: Open Court, 1999.

—*Later Mohist Logic, Ethics and Science*. Hong Kong: Chinese University Press, 2003.

Guo, Qiyong. *Contemporary New Confucianism II*. London: Routledge, 2023.

Guorong, Yang. *The Mutual Cultivation of Self and Things: A Contemporary Chinese Philosophy of the Meaning of Being*. Translated by Chad Austin Meyers. Bloomington: Indiana University Press, 2016.

Haldane, Elizabeth Sanderson. *James Frederick Ferrier*. Bristol: Thoemmes Continuum, 1992.

Hall, J. Storrs. *Where Is My Flying Car?* San Francisco: Stripe Press, 2021.

Hampson, Margaret. 'Imitating Virtue'. *Phronesis* 64, 3 (4 June 2019): 292–320.

Han, Byung-Chul. *The Transparency Society*. Stanford: Stanford Briefs, 2015.

Han, Suyin. *A Many-Splendoured Thing*. Harmondsworth: Penguin, 1959.

—*My House Has Two Doors*. London: Jonathan Cape, 1980.

Hansen, Chad. *A Daoist Theory of Chinese Thought: A Philosophical Interpretation*. New York: Oxford University Press, 2000.

—'A Tao of Tao in Chuang-Tzu'. In *Experimental Essays on Chuang-Tzu*. Edited by Victor Mair, 24–55. Honolulu: University of Hawaii Press, 1983.

—'Daoism'. In *The Stanford Encyclopedia of Philosophy*. Edited by Edward N. Zalta and Uri Nodelman, Summer 2024. Stanford: Metaphysics Research Lab, Stanford University, 2024. https://plato.stanford.edu/archives/sum2024/entries/daoism/.

Harvey, Jerry. 'The Abilene Paradox: The Management of Agreement'. *Organizational Dynamics* 3, 1 (1 June 1974): 63–80.

Haven, Cynthia. *Evolution of Desire: A Life of René Girard*. East Lansing: Michigan State University Press, 2018.

He, Fan. 'The Evolution of Xuantong in Early Daoist Philosophy'. *Asian Philosophy* 34, 2 (2 April 2024): 120–35.

Hirsch, Eli. *Dividing Reality*. New York: Oxford University Press, 1997.

Hobsbawm, Eric, and Terence Ranger, eds. *The Invention of Tradition*. Cambridge: Cambridge University Press, 1992.

Hogan, Patrick Colm. *The Culture of Conformism: Understanding Social Consent*. Durham: Duke University Press, 2001.

Holland, Tom. *Dominion: The Making of the Western Mind*. London: Abacus, 2020.

Hu, Shih. *The Development of the Logical Method in Ancient China*. Shanghai: Oriental Book Company, 1922.

Hua, An Li King Of. *Essential Huainanzi: Liu An, King of Huainan*. Translated by Sarah Queen, Andrew Seth Meyer, Harold Roth and John Major. New York: Columbia University Press, 2012.

Hua, Yu. *China in Ten Words*. London: Duckworth, 2012.

Hunter, Graeme. *Radical Protestantism in Spinoza's Thought*. London: Routledge, 2017.

Illich, Ivan, and David Cayley. *The Rivers North of the Future: The Testament of Ivan Illich*. Toronto: House of Anansi, 2005.

Israel, Jonathan. *Democratic Enlightenment: Philosophy, Revolution, and Human Rights 1750–1790*. Oxford: Oxford University Press, 2013.

—*Enlightenment Contested: Philosophy, Modernity, and the Emancipation of Man 1670–1752*. Oxford: Oxford University Press, 2006.

—*Radical Enlightenment: Philosophy and the Making of Modernity 1650–1750*. Oxford: Oxford University Press, 2002.

—*The Enlightenment That Failed: Ideas, Revolution, and Democratic Defeat, 1748–1830*. Oxford: Oxford University Press, 2019.

Israel, Prof. Jonathan I. *Spinoza, Life and Legacy*. Oxford: Oxford University Press, 2023.

Ivanhoe, Philip J., and Bryan W. Van Norden, eds. *Readings in Classical Chinese Philosophy*. Indianapolis: Hackett, 2006.

Izutsu, Toshihiko. *Sufism and Taoism: A Comparative Study of Key Philosophical Concepts*. Berkeley: University of California Press, 2016.

James, Lawrence. *The Lion and the Dragon: Britain and China: A History of Conflict*. London: Weidenfeld & Nicolson, 2023.

James, Susan. *Spinoza on Learning to Live Together*. Oxford: Oxford University Press, 2020.

Jarrett, Charles. 'Spinozistic Constructivism'. In *Essays on Spinoza's Ethical Theory*. Edited by Matthew Kisner and Andrew Youpa. Oxford: Oxford University Press, 2014.

Jiang, Tao. 'Isaiah Berlin's Challenge to the Zhuangzian Freedom'. *Journal of Chinese Philosophy* 39, S1 (2012): 69–92.

Kamal, Muhammad. 'Ibn 'Arabi and Spinoza on God and the World'. *Open Journal of Philosophy* 7, 4 (15 September 2017): 409–21.

Kaplan, Benjamin. *Calvinists and Libertines: Confession and Community in Utrecht 1578–1620*. Oxford: Oxford University Press, 1995.

Kasser, Tim. *The High Price of Materialism*. Cambridge, MA: MIT Press, 2003.

Kierkegaard, Søren. *The Sickness Unto Death: A Christian Psychological Exposition of Edification and Awakening by Anti-Climacus*. Translated by Alastair Hannay. London: Penguin Classics, 1989.

Kirwan, Michael. *Discovering Girard*. Cambridge: Cowley Publications, 2005.

Klein, Esther. 'Were There "Inner Chapters" in the Warring States? A New Examination of Evidence about the Zhuangzi'. *T'oung Pao* 96, 4 (1 January 2010): 299–369.

Klostermaier, Klaus. *A Survey of Hinduism*. Third edition. New York: SUNY Press, 2007.

Knaul, Livia. 'Kuo Hsiang and the Chuang Tzu'. *Journal of Chinese Philosophy* 12, 4 (1985): 429–47.

Ko, Young Woon. *The Non-Hierarchical Way from Yijing to Jeongyeok: A New Paradigm for East Meeting West*. Lanham: Lexington Books, 2022.

Korsgaard, Christine. *The Sources of Normativity*. Cambridge: Cambridge University Press, 1996.

Lai, Karyn. *An Introduction to Chinese Philosophy*. Cambridge: Cambridge University Press, 2017.

—'Freedom and Agency in the Zhuangzi: Navigating Life's Constraints'. *British Journal for the History of Philosophy* 30, 1 (2 January 2022): 3–23.

Landy, Joshua. 'Deceit, Desire, and the Literature Professor: Why Girardians Exist'. *Republic of Letters* 1, 3 (2012): 1–21.

Laozi. *Daodejing*. Translated by Brook Ziporyn. New York: W. W. Norton & Co., 2023.

—*Daodejing: The New, Highly Readable Translation of the Life-Changing Ancient Scripture Formerly Known as the Tao Te Ching*. Translated by Hans-Georg Moeller. Chicago: Open Court, 2007.

Lear, Jonathan. *Radical Hope: Ethics in the Face of Cultural Devastation*. Cambridge, MA: Harvard University Press, 2008.

Leavy, Mark. *The Curse of the Self: Self-Awareness, Egotism, and the Quality of Human Life*. Oxford: Oxford University Press, 2004.

Lee, Gregory. 'Au-delà des limites: pour un nouvel imaginaire culturel'. *Transtext(e)s Transcultures 跨文本跨文化. Journal of Global Cultural Studies*, 13 (1 December 2018).

—*China Imagined: From European Fantasy to Spectacular Power*. Oxford: Oxford University Press, 2018.

Li, Chenyang. *The Tao Encounters the West: Explorations in Comparative Philosophy*. Albany: SUNY Press, 1999.

Lin, Yutang. *The Importance of Living*. New York: William Morrow, 1998.

Lo, Yuet Keung. 'The Authorship of the Zhuangzi'. In *Dao Companion to the Philosophy of the Zhuangzi*. Edited by Kim-chong Chong, 43–97. Dao Companions to Chinese Philosophy. Cham: Springer International Publishing, 2022.

Longenecker, Michael Tze-Sung. 'On Becoming a Rooster: Zhuangzian Conventionalism and the Survival of Death'. *Dao* 21, 1 (1 March 2022): 61–79.

Lubis, Mochtar. *Twilight in Jakarta*. London: Darf, 2017.

Lynn, Richard John, trans. *Zhuangzi: A New Translation of the Sayings of Master Zhuang as Interpreted by Guo Xiang*. New York: Columbia University Press, 2022.

Maalouf, Amin. *In the Name of Identity*. New York: Arcade Publishing, 2012.

Mahtani, Shibani, and Anna Fifield. '"You Will Never Hear Me Mention His Name": New Zealand's Ardern Vows to Deny Accused Shooter Notoriety'. *Washington Post*, 19 March 2019. https://www.washingtonpost.com/world/asia_pacific/you-will-never-hear-me-mention-his-name-new-zealands-ardern-hopes-to-deny-shooter-notoriety/2019/03/19/b4d163b8-49b5-11e9-8cfc-2c5d0999c21e_story.html.

Marwick, Alice. *Status Update: Celebrity, Publicity, and Branding in the Social Media Age*. New Haven: Yale University Press, 2015.

Masters, Blake, and Peter Thiel. *Zero to One: Notes on Start Ups, or How to Build the Future*. London: Virgin Books, 2015.

Matheron, Alexandre. *Individu et communauté chez Spinoza*. Paris: Éditions de Minuit, 1969.

—*Politics, Ontology and Knowledge in Spinoza*. Edited by Filippo Del Lucchese, David Maruzella and Gil Morejón. Translated by David

Maruzella and Gil Morejón. Edinburgh: Edinburgh University Press, 2020.

Maurer, Armand. *Medieval Philosophy*. Edited by Étienne Gilson. Toronto: Pontifical Institute of Mediaeval Studies, 1982.

McCloskey, Deirdre. *Why Liberalism Works: How True Liberal Values Produce a Freer, More Equal, Prosperous World for All*. New Haven: Yale University Press, 2019.

Mercier, Hugo. *Not Born Yesterday: The Science of Who We Trust and What We Believe*. Princeton University Press, 2020.

Mishra, Pankaj. *Age of Anger: A History of the Present*. New York: Farrar, Straus and Giroux, 2017.

—*Run and Hide*. London: Penguin, 2023.

Mo, Timothy. *An Insular Possession*. London: Paddleless Press, 2002.

Moeller, Hans-Georg, and Paul D'Ambrosio. *Genuine Pretending: On the Philosophy of the Zhuangzi*. New York: Columbia University Press, 2017.

—*You and Your Profile: Identity After Authenticity*. New York: Columbia University Press, 2021.

Mormino, Gianfranco. 'Dal desiderio infantile alla religione: Spinoza e Girard'. In *René Girard e la filosofia*. Edited by Giuseppe Fornari and Gianfranco Mormino, 29–42. Milan: Filosofie, 2012.

Morris, Ian, Margaret Atwood, Christine M. Korsgaard, Richard Seaford and Jonathan D. Spence. *Foragers, Farmers, and Fossil Fuels: How Human Values Evolve*. Edited by Stephen Macedo. Princeton: Princeton University Press, 2015.

Morrison, John. 'Two Puzzles about Thought and Identity in Spinoza'. In *Cambridge Critical Guide to Spinoza's Ethics*. Edited by Yitzhak Melamed, 56–81, 2017.

Murdoch, Iris. *Existentialists and Mystics*. New York: Allen Lane, 1998.

Nadler, Steven. *Spinoza's Heresy: Immortality and the Jewish Mind*. Oxford: Oxford University Press, 2004.

Nadler, Steven M. *Spinoza: A Life*. Cambridge: Cambridge University Press, 2001.

Naipaul, Vidiadhar Surajprasad. *Among the Believers: An Islamic Journey*. London: Picador, 2010.

—*Beyond Belief: Islamic Excursions among the Converted Peoples*. London: Abacus, 1999.

—*The Mimic Men*. Reprints edition. London: Picador, 2011.

Naughton, John. 'Steve Jobs: Stanford Commencement Address, June 2005'. *Observer*, 8 October 2011, sec. Technology. https://www.theguardian.com/technology/2011/oct/09/steve-jobs-stanford-commencement-address.

Neville, Robert. *God the Creator: On the Transcendence and Presence of God*. Albany: State University of New York Press, 1992.

Nevzlin, Irina. *The Impact of Identity: The Power of Knowing Who You Are*. Independently Published, 2019.

Nylan, Michael. 'Academic Silos, or, "What I Wish Philosophers Knew about History in Early China"'. In *The Bloomsbury Research Handbook of Chinese Philosophy Methodologies*. Edited by Sor-hoon Tan, 91–114. London: Bloomsbury, 2017.

Olberding, Amy. *Moral Exemplars in the Analects: The Good Person is That*. New York: Routledge, 2011.

Oughourlian, Jean-Michel. *The Puppet of Desire: The Psychology of Hysteria, Possession, and Hypnosis*. Stanford: Stanford University Press, 1991.

Özbey, Sonya N. *Different Beasts: Humans and Animals in Spinoza and the Zhuangzi*. New York: Oxford University Press, 2024.

Ozeki, Ruth. *The Face: A Time Code*. Brooklyn: Restless Books, 2016.

Palaver, Wolfgang. *René Girard's Mimetic Theory*. East Lansing: Michigan State University Press, 2013.

Paley, Chris. *Beyond Bad: How Obsolete Morals are Holding Us Back*. London: Coronet, 2021.

Pascal, Blaise. *Pensées and Other Writings*. Edited by Anthony Levi. Translated by Honor Levi. Oxford: Oxford University Press, 2008.

Phelps, Edmund. *Mass Flourishing: How Grassroots Innovation Created Jobs, Challenge, and Change*. Reprint edition. Princeton: Princeton University Press, 2015.

Phelps, Edmund, Gylfi Zoega, Hian Teck Hoon and Raicho Bojilov. *A Vital People: Testing the Theory of Innovation: The Values That Drive Innovation, Job Satisfaction, and Economic Growth*. Cambridge, MA: Harvard University Press, 2020.

Pogue, James. 'Inside the New Right, Where Peter Thiel is Placing His Biggest Bets'. *Vanity Fair*, 20 April 2022. https://www.vanityfair.com/news/2022/04/inside-the-new-right-where-peter-thiel-is-placing-his-biggest-bets.

Reu, Wim De. 'A Ragbag of Odds and Ends? Argument Structure and Philosophical Coherence in Zhuangzi 26'. In *Literary Forms of Argument in Early China*, by Joachim Genz and Dirk Meyer, 243–96. Leiden: Brill, 2015.

Reu, Wim De. 'The Unresponsive Fighting Cocks : Mastery and Human Interaction in the Zhuangzi'. In *Skill and Mastery Philosophical Stories from the Zhuangzi*. Edited by Karyn Lai and Wai Wai Chiu. London: Rowman & Littlefield International, 2019.

Ridley, Matt. *How Innovation Works*. New York: Harper Perennial, 2020.

Ritchie, Hannah. *Not the End of the World: How We Can Be the First Generation to Build a Sustainable Planet*. London: Vintage, 2024.

Robinson, Joan. *The Cultural Revolution in China*. London: Penguin, 1969.

Sartre, Jean-Paul. *Being and Nothingness*. Translated by Sarah Richmond. Abingdon: Routledge, 2018.

—*Existentialism is a Humanism*. Translated by Carol Macomber. New Haven: Yale University Press, 2007.

Saunders Jr, Frank. 'Primitivism in the Zhuangzi: An Introduction'. *Philosophy Compass* 15, 10 (2020).

Sen, Amartya. *Identity and Violence: The Illusion of Destiny*. New York: W. W. Norton, 2007.

Shapiro, Lisa. 'Self-Consciousness and Consciousness of Self: Spinoza on Desire and Pride'. In *Mind, Body, and Morality: New Perspectives on Descartes and Spinoza*. Edited by Martina Reuter and Frans Svensson, 143–56. London: Routledge, 2019.

Sinclair, May. *A Defence of Idealism: Some Questions and Conclusions*. London: Macmillan, 1917. http://archive.org/details/adefenceidealis02sincgoog.

Sinclair, Upton. *I, Candidate for Governor and How I Got Licked*. Berkeley: University of California Press, 1994.

Souza, Joanne, and Paul Bingham. *Death from a Distance and the Birth of a Humane Universe: Human Evolution, Behavior, History, and Your Future*. BookSurge, 2009.

Spinoza, Benedict. *Oeuvres*. Edited by Fokke Akkerman. Translated by Jacqueline Lagrée and Pierre-François Moreau. Vol. 3. Paris: Presses Universitaires de France, 2012.

—*Oeuvres*. Edited by Fokke Akkerman and Piet Steenbakkers. Translated by Pierre-François Moreau. Vol. 4. Paris: Presses Universitaires de France, 2020.

Spinoza, Benedictus de. *Opera*. Edited by Carl Gebhardt. Heidelberg: Carl Winter, 1925.

—*The Collected Works of Spinoza*. Translated by Edwin Curley. Vol. 1. Princeton: Princeton University Press, 1985.

Srinivasan, Amia. *The Right to Sex*. London: Bloomsbury Publishing, 2022.

Storr, Will. *Selfie: How the West Became Self-Obsessed*. London: Picador, 2018.

—*The Status Game: On Human Life and How to Play It*. London: William Collins, 2021.

Strohminger, Nina, and Shaun Nichols. 'The Essential Moral Self'. *Cognition* 131, 1 (April 2014): 159–71.

Sunstein, Cass. *Conformity: The Power of Social Influences*. New York: NYU Press, 2019.

Tagore, Rabindranath. *Creative Unity*. London: Macmillan, 1922.

—*Gora*. Translated by Radha Chakravarty. London: Penguin, 2009.

—*The Essential Tagore*. Cambridge, MA: Harvard University Press, 2011.

—*The Religion of Man: Being the Hibbert Lectures for 1930*. London: Allen & Unwin, 1958.

Tan, Christine Abigail. 'Guo Xiang's Ontology of Zide'. *Monumenta Serica* 69, 1 (2 January 2021): 1–17.

—'The Butterfly Dream and Zhuangzi's Perspectivism: An Exploration of Differing Interpretations of the Butterfly Dream Against the Backdrop of Dao as Pluralistic Monism'. *Kritike* 10, 2 (2016): 100–121.

Tawney, Richard Henry. *Religion and the Rise of Capitalism*. London: Penguin, 1948.

Taylor, Alan John Percivale. *Europe: Grandeur and Decline*. Harmondsworth: Penguin, 1967.

Trilling, Lionel. *Sincerity and Authenticity*. Cambridge, MA: Harvard University Press, 1972.

Unamuno, Miguel de. *Tragic Sense of Life*. Translated by J. E. C. Flitch. New York: Dover, 2000.

United Nations. 'Human Development Report 2023–24: Breaking the Gridlock: Reimagining Cooperation in a Polarized World'. United Nations, 13 March 2024. https://hdr.undp.org/content/human-development-report-2023-24.

Vogelsang, Kai. *Introduction to Classical Chinese*. Oxford: Oxford University Press, 2021.

Waugh, Evelyn. *Decline and Fall*. London: Penguin Classics, 2001.

Weil, Simone. *First and Last Notebooks: Supernatural Knowledge*. Eugene: Wipf and Stock, 2015.

Whitman, Walt. *Democratic Vistas*. New York: Smith & McDougal, 1871.

Wiggins, David. 'Deliberation and Practical Reason'. *Proceedings of the Aristotelian Society* 76 (1975): 29–51.

Wilde, Oscar. *De Profundis*. London: Methuen, 1915.

Wolf, Susan. 'The Meanings of Lives'. In *The Variety of Values: Essays on Morality, Meaning, and Love*. Oxford: Oxford University Press, 2015.

Wood, Ellen Meiksins. *The Origin of Capitalism: A Longer View*. London: Verso, 2016.

Wrangham, Richard. *The Goodness Paradox: The Strange Relationship Between Virtue and Violence in Human Evolution*. New York: Vintage, 2019.

Wu, Kuang-Ming. *Chuang-Tzu: World Philosopher at Play*. New York: Crossroads, 1982.

—*The Butterfly as Companion: Meditations on the First Three Chapters of the Chuang Tzu*. Albany: State University of New York Press, 1990.

Xu, Xi. *This Fish Is Fowl: Essays of Being*. Lincoln: University of Nebraska Press, 2019.

Yao, Zhihua. ' "I Have Lost Me": Zhuangzi's Butterfly Dream'. *Journal of Chinese Philosophy* 40, 3–4 (2013): 511–26.

Yovel, Yirmiyahu. *Spinoza and Other Heretics, Volume 1: The Marrano of Reason*. Princeton: Princeton University Press, 2021.

Yu, Jiyuan. *The Ethics of Confucius and Aristotle: Mirrors of Virtue*. New York: Routledge, 2013.

Yunkaporta, Tyson. *Sand Talk: How Indigenous Thinking Can Save the World*. Melbourne: Text Publishing Company, 2020.

Zhang, Ellen. 'The "Greening" of Daoism: Potential and Limits'. *Asian Studies* 11, 2 (16 May 2023): 69–94.

Zheng, Kai. *The Metaphysics of Philosophical Daoism*. London: Routledge, 2020.

Zhu, Xi. *Sishu zhangju ji zhu* 四書章句集注 [*Annotations to the Four Books*]. Beijing: Zhonghua shuju, 2012.

Zhuangzi. *Chuang Tzu: The Inner Chapters*. Translated by A. C. Graham. London: Mandala, 1986.

—*Zhuangzi: The Complete Writings: The Complete Writings*. Translated by Brook Ziporyn. Indianapolis: Hackett, 2020.

Zhuangzi, and Yu-lan Fung. *Chuang-Tzu: A New Selected Translation with an Exposition of the Philosophy of Kuo Hsiang*. Berlin: Springer, 2015.

Ziporyn, Brook. *Emptiness and Omnipresence: An Essential Introduction to Tiantai Buddhism*. Bloomington: Indiana University Press, 2016.

—*Ironies of Oneness and Difference: Coherence in Early Chinese Thought; Prolegomena to the Study of Li*. New York: SUNY Press, 2012.

—*The Penumbra Unbound: The Neo-Taoist Philosophy of Guo Xiang*. Albany: State University of New York Press, 2003.

Notes

Introduction: Identity Kills

1 The concept of 'China' is a much more modern and Western invention, according to Gregory Lee: Lee, *China Imagined*.

2 Zhuangzi, *Chuang Tzu*, 98–9. The dumpling is written 餛飩 rather than 混沌 – the food radical (飠) replaces the water radical in the two characters.

3 Ibid.

4 Girardot, *Myth and Meaning in Early Daoism*, 75; Girard, *The Scapegoat*. An interesting comparison is with the figure of Purusha in Hindu mythology. He is sacrificed in order to create a world and is said to have 'embraced the earth on all sides' and to be 'this all, that which was and which shall be': Klostermaier, *A Survey of Hinduism*, 87.

5 Moeller and D'Ambrosio, *You and Your Profile*, 230. The complex significance of the face as a symbol of identity is explored in the series *The Face*, published by Restless Books: Ozeki, *The Face*; Abani, *The Face*; Aw, *The Face*.

6 Lynn, *Zhuangzi*, 174. This is not how it would have been pronounced in the past, but the convention today is to pronounce the language in which it was written as though its characters were the 'traditional' characters of modern Mandarin, as used in Taiwan. The language of the *Zhuangzi* is sometimes known as 'Classical Chinese', although 'Chinese' here is an anachronistic label. It is also known as *gu wen* 古文, *wen yan* 文言, or *wen yan wen* 文言文.

7 Augustine, *Confessions*, 2018, 10.50. In other editions this passage occurs at the end of Chapter 33 of Book 10.
8 Girard, *Battling to the End*, 18.
9 Baumeister, *The Self Explained*, 7.
10 The connection between identity and violence has been observed by many thinkers: Sen, *Identity and Violence*; Appiah, *The Lies That Bind*; Butler, *Giving an Account of Oneself*; Leavy, *The Curse of the Self*; Maalouf, *In the Name of Identity*.
11 Derrida, *Points . . .*, 340.
12 Moeller and D'Ambrosio, *You and Your Profile*, 230.
13 Appiah, *The Lies That Bind*, 10.
14 Matheron, *Individu et communauté*, 89.
15 Baumeister, *The Self Explained*, 322. Xu Xi's essay collection, *This Fish Is Fowl*, is a moving study of identity deficits arising from sources such as cultural displacement and Alzheimer's disease.
16 Wrangham, *The Goodness Paradox*.
17 Girardot, *Myth and Meaning in Early Daoism*, 77–8.
18 United Nations, 'Breaking the Gridlock'.
19 Ibid., 190.
20 The beliefs are 'reflective' rather than 'intuitive'; on this distinction see: Mercier, *Not Born Yesterday*, 152.
21 Nadler, *Spinoza's Heresy*; Nadler, *Spinoza*, chap. 6; Israel, *Spinoza, Life and Legacy*, chap. 3; Buruma, *Spinoza*, chap. 5; Goldstein, *Betraying Spinoza*, chap. 4.
22 Haven, *Evolution of Desire*, 28.
23 The historian A. J. P. Taylor once expressed incomprehension at the way figures like Hitler and Mussolini are commonly characterized as 'lunatics': 'All men are mad,' he wrote, 'who devote themselves to the pursuit of power when they could be fishing, painting pictures, or simply sitting in the sun' – Taylor, *Europe: Grandeur and Decline*, 221–2.
24 Lee, 'Au-delà des limites'; Zhang, 'The "Greening" of Daoism'.

1. 'The Perfect Person Has No Identity'

1 The *Dao De Jing* or *Tao Te Ching* 道德經 (Classic of the Way and Virtue) is a series of verses whose oldest parts go back to the fourth century BCE. It is ascribed to the ancient author Laozi 老子, a supposed contemporary of Confucius, and is the founding text of Daoism. It is the second-most translated text in the world, after the Bible. See Chan, 'The Daode Jing and Its Tradition'.

2 Hansen, 'Daoism'.

3 Graham, *Disputers of the Tao*, 172.

4 Zhuangzi, *Chuang Tzu*, 128.

5 Klein, 'Were There "Inner Chapters" in the Warring States?'; Lo, 'The Authorship of the Zhuangzi'.

6 Chan, 'Neo-Daoism'. François Billeter is highly critical of Guo Xiang's commentary, which he takes to distort Zhuangzi's meaning: 'transforming a thought of radical autonomy, personal independence, and refusal of servitude and domination into an apology for disengagement and moral indifference – a form of nonchalance that allowed the aristocrats of their times to serve the powers in place, despite the disgust they inspired'. Billeter, *Leçons sur Tchouang-tseu*, 130. I believe this to overlook the extent to which disengagement and nonchalance are a way to escape from servitude in both the *Zhuangzi* and Guo's commentary.

7 Graham, *Disputers of the Tao*, 174; Zhuangzi, *Chuang Tzu*, 3–4; Zhuangzi, *Zhuangzi*, xxi–xxii.

8 Henceforth all citations in this format are to Richard John Lynn's translation of Guo Xiang's edition of the *Zhuangzi*: Lynn, *Zhuangzi*.

9 Graham, *Disputers of the Tao*, 4.

10 Von Falkenhausen, 'The Economy of Late Pre-Imperial China', 18.

11 Özbey, *Different Beasts*, 23.

12 Hu, *The Development of the Logical Method in Ancient China*, 3.

13 Confucius, *The Analects of Confucius*, 12:11.

14 Zhu, *Sishu zhangju ji zhu* 四書章句集注 [Annotations to the *Four Books*], 136; Moeller and D'Ambrosio, *Genuine Pretending*, 46.

15 Hu, *The Development of the Logical Method in Ancient China*, 3.

16 Graham, *Disputers of the Tao*, 4.

17 Yu, *Ethics of Confucius and Aristotle*, 41.

18 Confucius, *The Analects of Confucius*, 13:3.

19 Moeller and D'Ambrosio, *Genuine Pretending*, 43.

20 Yu, *Ethics of Confucius and Aristotle*, 41.

21 Moeller and D'Ambrosio, *Genuine Pretending*, 46.

22 Some readers might recognize the figure of *Meng mu* 孟母 – the mother of the philosopher Mencius, who plays a symbolic role as an exemplar of maternity.

23 Moeller and D'Ambrosio, *Genuine Pretending*, chap. 2; Trilling, *Sincerity and Authenticity*.

24 Moeller and D'Ambrosio, *You and Your Profile*, chap. 3.

25 Hogan, *Culture of Conformism*; Sunstein, *Conformity*.

26 There is some discussion of what happens to roles in a time of 'cultural devastation' in Lear, *Radical Hope*.

27 Saunders Jr, 'Primitivism in the Zhuangzi'.

28 Yao, 'I Have Lost Me', 519. What Yao means is that the character *wo* 我 is composed of *shou* 手, 'hand', and *ge* 戈, 'dagger-axe'.

29 I will use the characters 吾 and 我 liberally in what follows, to keep this pictorial association in mind. The reader may pronounce them in her mind however she sees fit (the standard practice of using modern Mandarin pronunciations is a matter of convenience).

30 Anscombe, 'The First Person'.

31 Wu, *The Butterfly as Companion*, chap. 2; Tan, 'Butterfly Dream', 114–17.

32 Vogelsang, *Introduction to Classical Chinese*, 24.
33 Wu, *The Butterfly as Companion*, 206.
34 Kierkegaard, *The Sickness Unto Death*, 101.
35 Murdoch, *Existentialists and Mystics*, 122–3.
36 Whitman, *Democratic Vistas*, 37–8.
37 The reference to Whitman might mislead the reader into thinking that individualism is peculiar to the culture of the United States of America, but note the positive assessment in Lin, *The Importance of Living*, chap. 4, §6.
38 The psychologist Roy Baumeister writes: 'You have to find a way to decide who you want to be. You need some criteria to sort among the many options,' and then: 'You need meta-criteria, higher-level criteria to decide which set of criteria you will use to decide who to be' – Baumeister, *The Self Explained*, 30.
39 Wu, *The Butterfly as Companion*, chap. 2.
40 Ibid., 206.
41 Zheng, *The Metaphysics of Philosophical Daoism*, 171.
42 Ibid.
43 Li, *The Tao Encounters the West*, 28–9.
44 Zheng, *The Metaphysics of Philosophical Daoism*, 171.
45 Izutsu, *Sufism and Taoism*, 358.
46 Ibid., 360.
47 Izutsu uses the term 'existentialism' for this, but this is too confusing in most Western philosophical contexts, where that term is already taken for something else.
48 Knaul, 'Kuo Hsiang and the Chuang Tzu', 439.
49 Ziporyn, *The Penumbra Unbound*, 59.
50 Ibid. If the '*wu*' here is meant to be 吾, this must be being used in a different sense from that which we have been taking from Kuang-Ming Wu, which seems to line up more with how Ziporyn understands *zi* 自.
51 Lynn, *Zhuangzi*, 23.19.5–6.

52 Ziporyn, *The Penumbra Unbound*, 59.

53 Chen, *In Praise of Nothing*, 134.

54 Moeller and D'Ambrosio, *Genuine Pretending*, Introduction; Ziporyn, *Ironies of Oneness and Difference*, chap. 4.

55 In Lynn's translation: 'the Perfected one has no self'. Lynn, *Zhuangzi*, 1.7.14.

2. *Avoid Footprints*

1 Mo, *An Insular Possession*, 566. The passage has been used as the epigram to a study of identity in the digital age: Moeller and D'Ambrosio, *You and Your Profile*.

2 Baumeister finds that: 'People feel most authentic when their actions fit with their desired reputations. "That's me!" is what they feel, elated because it is how they want to be known to others' – Baumeister, *The Self Explained*, 58.

3 Mo, *An Insular Possession*, 566.

4 'Hubris rather than opium led to the war between Britain and China in 1839' – James, *The Lion and the Dragon*, 3.

5 Olberding, *Moral Exemplars in the Analects*, 20–21.

6 Hua, *China in Ten Words*, 154.

7 The original passage from the *Zhuangzi*, '故意仁義其非人情乎！', is also translated to mean the opposite of what it is in Lynn; Ziporyn, e.g., has 'human kindness and responsible conduct are not the uncontrived condition of man!' Zhuangzi, *Zhuangzi*, 78–9.

8 Zhuangzi and Fung, *Chuang-Tzu*, 63. Some of the ideas here are drawn from the pioneering scholar Feng Youlan (1895–1990): Guo, *Contemporary New Confucianism II*, chap. 2.

9 Olberding, *Moral Exemplars in the Analects*, 20–21.

10 Zhuangzi and Fung, *Chuang-Tzu*, 63.

11 Moeller and D'Ambrosio, *Genuine Pretending*, 34–40.

12 Ziporyn, *The Penumbra Unbound*, 59.

13 Lai, *An Introduction to Chinese Philosophy*, 98; Nylan, 'Academic Silos, or, "What I Wish Philosophers Knew about History in Early China" ', 98.

14 Zhuangzi, *Zhuangzi*, 287. The square-bracket additions are Ziporyn's. Lynn, whose translation I generally rely on, consistently translates *youwei* 有為 as 'selfconscious action' and *wuwei* 無為 as 'unselfconscious action'.

15 Wu, *The Butterfly as Companion*, 206.

16 Jiang, 'Isaiah Berlin's Challenge to the Zhuangzian Freedom'; Lai, 'Freedom and Agency in the Zhuangzi'. See also the discussion of *laozhe* 勞者 versus *yizhe* 佚者 in Reu, 'Ragbag'.

17 Is it perhaps relevant that Zhuangzi might have been himself a gardener of the lacquer forest?

18 The line comes from Laozi, *Daodejing*, 2007; Laozi, *Daodejing*, 2023.

19 Ziporyn, *The Penumbra Unbound*, 66–7.

20 Zigong's failure to 'understand the arts of Mr. Hundun is due to [his] acceptance of the values of face and "fame" ' – Girardot, *Myth and Meaning in Early Daoism*, 80.

21 He, 'The Evolution of Xuantong in Early Daoist Philosophy'.

22 Ziporyn, *The Penumbra Unbound*, 66.

23 Ibid., 67.

24 Naipaul, *Among the Believers*, 332.

25 Naipaul, *The Mimic Men*.

26 Mishra, *Age of Anger*, 266.

27 Naipaul, *Beyond Belief*.

28 Mishra, *Age of Anger*, 266.

29 Ibid., 290.

30 Mahtani and Fifield, 'You Will Never Hear Me Mention His Name'.

31 Bootle, *This Is Not Who I Am*, 88.

32 Ibid., 86.

33 Ibid., 85.

3. Nothing in Particular

1 Appiah, *The Lies That Bind*, 219.

2 Ibid.

3 Sen, *Identity and Violence*, 38.

4 Ibid., 39.

5 The story of Karen Templer, recounted by Storr, might be instructive here. Storr, *The Status Game*, chap. 19.

6 Tagore, *Gora*, 1.

7 Tagore, *Creative Unity*, 36.

8 'On the Day Thou Breakst Through This My Name': Tagore, *The Essential Tagore*, 257.

9 Moses ben Maimon (1138–1204), known as Maimonides, sought to harmonize Aristotle's teaching with the tenets of Jewish faith. It is said that the Caliph al-Ma'mūn 'embarked on his reforming initiative after Aristotle appeared to him in a dream' – Campanini, *An Introduction to Islamic Philosophy*, 42. And although Aristotelianism was condemned by the Catholic church in 1277, it soon after became the theological foundation of Western Christianity with its greatest Christian expounder, Thomas Aquinas, canonized in 1323 and declared a Doctor of the Church in 1567 – Maurer, *Medieval Philosophy*, 275, 529n275.

10 Storr, *Selfie*, 134.

11 Chen, *In Praise of Nothing*, 133.

12 Ibid., 134.

13 Ibid.

14 Wilde, *De Profundis*, 71–2.

15 Izutsu, *Sufism and Taoism*, 360.

16 Ibid.

17 Graham, *Later Mohist Logic, Ethics and Science*, 26.

18 Chan, *A Source Book in Chinese Philosophy*, 235–7; Ivanhoe and Norden, *Readings in Classical Chinese Philosophy*, 363–8; Graham, *Disputers of the Tao*, 85–95.

19 Ziporyn, *Ironies of Oneness and Difference*, 170.

20 The point is carefully explained and argued in Hirsch, *Dividing Reality*.

21 Tan, 'Butterfly Dream', 119.

22 Longenecker, 'On Becoming a Rooster'.

23 This is suggested in the commentary of Chen Guying: Chen, *The Philosophy of Life*, 29.

24 Eddington, *Nature of the Physical World*, 31–8.

25 Although if you are interested you can start with: Hansen, 'A Tao of Tao in Chuang-Tzu'; Allinson, 'On the Question of Relativism in the Chuang-Tzu'; Chinn, 'Zhuangzi and Relativistic Scepticism'; Tan, 'Butterfly Dream'; Cantor, 'Zhuangzi on "Happy Fish" and the Limits of Human Knowledge'.

26 Chen, *The Philosophy of Life*, 23.

27 ASEAN is the Association of Southeast Asian Nations (https://asean.org/). Appiah does not specify who he means by this rather blanket epithet, so I have suggested President Suharto as an example near enough to the publication of the first edition of Appiah's book (2005).

28 Appiah, *The Ethics of Identity*, 247.

29 Ibid., 253.

30 Reu, 'The Unresponsive Fighting Cocks'.

31 Chen, *The Philosophy of Life*, 31.

32 Lynn, *Zhuangzi*, 2.10.9.

33 Ziporyn, *Ironies of Oneness and Difference*, 175; Hansen, *A Daoist Theory of Chinese Thought*, 283.

34 Tan, 'Butterfly Dream', 119.

35 Morris et al., *Foragers, Farmers, and Fossil Fuels*, 253.

36 Paley, *Beyond Bad*, chap. 5; Baumeister, *The Self Explained*, chap. 9; Wrangham, *The Goodness Paradox*, chap. 10.

37 Guorong, *The Mutual Cultivation of Self and Things*. Guorong presents what might be taken as a contemporary version of Confucian exemplarism – a highly modified version, having incorporated a significant amount of Heideggerian thought.

38 Strohminger and Nichols, 'The Essential Moral Self', 169. See also Paley, *Beyond Bad*, 98–9; Baumeister, *The Self Explained*, 111–12. Moeller and D'Ambrosio's study of modern identity quotes the laconic, troubled detective Rustin Cohle from the series *True Detective* (S01, E08): 'As sentient meat, however illusory our identities are, we craft those identities by making value judgements': Moeller and D'Ambrosio, *You and Your Profile*, 26.

39 Maalouf, *In the Name of Identity*, 11–12.

40 Wu, *Chuang-Tzu*, 94.

41 Hua, *Essential Huainanzi*, 193.

42 Hua, *China in Ten Words*, 92.

43 Lai, 'Freedom and Agency in the Zhuangzi', 10.

44 Yunkaporta, *Sand Talk*, 54.

45 Ibid., 99.

46 Wolf, 'The Meanings of Lives', 100.

47 Yunkaporta, *Sand Talk*, 40.

4. *Persevering in Your Being*

1 Spinoza was not exactly an ordinary European, and we have very little to go on when we wonder what his attitudes towards colonialism would have been. See Diefenbach, 'Hallucinating Colonialism'.

2 Letter to Balzac, 5 May 1631, AT 1.203–4, CSM 3.31–2. 'AT' here and henceforth refers to Descartes, *Oeuvres*. 'CSM' refers to the English translation: Descartes, *Philosophical Writings*.

3 AT 1.204, CSM 3.32.

4 Tawney, *Religion and the Rise of Capitalism*, 35–6.

5 Tawney, 183.

6 Spinoza, *Tractatus Theologico-Politicus*, 3:504. All translations of Spinoza are mine.

7 Ibid., 3:506.

8 Tawney, *Religion and the Rise of Capitalism*, 74.

9 Wood, *Origin of Capitalism*, 57.

10 Ibid., 59.

11 Spinoza, *Tractatus Theologico-Politicus*, 3:184.

12 As Graeme Hunter points out, 'Spinoza's early life in the Jewish Community of Amsterdam and his later expulsion from it made him an outsider to the European mainstream. Still, it would be strange if he reflected as little of the religious temper of his own time as is commonly supposed.' Hunter, *Radical Protestantism in Spinoza's Thought*, 1.

13 Kaplan, *Calvinists and Libertines: Confession and Community in Utrecht 1578–1620*, 5.

14 Ibid., 6.

15 Trilling, *Sincerity and Authenticity*, 13.

16 Yovel, *Marrano of Reason*, 19.

17 Trilling, *Sincerity and Authenticity*, 10–11.

18 Bootle, *This Is Not Who I Am*, 2.

19 The biographical information here is drawn from various sources, including Feuer, *Spinoza and the Rise of Liberalism*; Nadler, *Spinoza*; Goldstein, *Betraying Spinoza*; Yovel, *Marrano of Reason*; Carlisle, *Spinoza's Religion*; Israel, *Spinoza, Life and Legacy*; Buruma, *Spinoza*.

20 Hunter, *Radical Protestantism in Spinoza's Thought*.
21 Spinoza, *The Collected Works of Spinoza*, 1:361.
22 Goldstein, *Betraying Spinoza*, 68.
23 All references of this form are to the *Ethics*: '3p6' means Proposition 6 of Part Three. The edition used is: Spinoza, *Ethica*. All translations are mine.
24 '3p9s' means scholium to Proposition 9 of Part Three.
25 Shapiro, 'Self-Consciousness and Consciousness of Self', 146.
26 Waugh, *Decline and Fall*, part 3, chap. 2.
27 Korsgaard, *The Sources of Normativity*, 117.
28 This means Appendix to Part Three, §1
29 Aquinas, *Summa Theologica*, 1a.q5.a5.ad3um. See Chapter 3, note 9 above.
30 Matheron, *Individu et communauté*, 89.
31 Nevzlin, *The Impact of Identity*, 20.
32 Ibid., 28.
33 Ibid., 36.
34 Ibid., 36.
35 Goldstein, *Betraying Spinoza*, chap. 4. The title of this chapter is 'Identity Crisis'.
36 Douglas, 'The Affects'; Douglas, 'Spinoza and Social Science'; Douglas, 'Spinoza, Money, and Desire'; Douglas, 'Spinoza's Unquiet Acquiescentia'; Douglas, *Philosophy of Hope*, chs. 2–3.
37 Aristotle (*Rhetoric* 2.11) describes emulation (*zēlos*) in somewhat similar terms, though he speaks of a *distress* at lacking what others 'like us by nature' (*homious tē phusei*) possess rather than of a desire for what they possess – see Hampson, 'Imitating Virtue', 305.
38 Translation from the Revised Oxford Edition: Aristotle, *Complete Works of Aristotle*.
39 Corollary to Proposition 31 of Part Three.
40 Part Four, Definitions of the Affects, §30.

5. The Fall

1 Baumeister, *The Self Explained*, 113.
2 Wrangham, *The Goodness Paradox*.
3 Ibid., 128.
4 Souza and Bingham, *Death from a Distance*.
5 Wrangham, *The Goodness Paradox*, 164ff.
6 Ibid., 149.
7 Girardot, *Myth and Meaning in Early Daoism*, 74; Moeller and D'Ambrosio, *You and Your Profile*, 229–32.
8 Storr, *The Status Game*, chap. 19.
9 Matheron, *Politics, Ontology and Knowledge in Spinoza*, chap. 9.
10 Spinoza, *Tractatus Theologico-Politicus*, vol. 3, chap. 16.
11 *Tractatus Politics*, chap. 1, §7. Spinoza, *Opera*, 3.276.
12 Collingwood, *The New Leviathan; Or, Man, Society, Civilization and Barbarism*, 36.73.
13 *Tractatus Politics*, chap. 6, §1. Spinoza, *Opera*, 3.297.
14 Matheron, *Politics, Ontology and Knowledge in Spinoza*, 126.
15 *Tractatus Politics*, chap. 3, §9. Spinoza, *Opera*, 3.288.
16 Matheron, *Politics, Ontology and Knowledge in Spinoza*, 128.
17 Matheron, *Individu et communauté*, 173–9.
18 Matheron, *Politics, Ontology and Knowledge in Spinoza*, 129.
19 Ibid., 130.
20 Dumouchel, *The Barren Sacrifice*, xiv.
21 Matheron, *Politics, Ontology and Knowledge in Spinoza*, 133.
22 Bourke, *The Second World War*, 155.
23 Debray, 'Imitation des affects et production de l'ordre social', 162.
24 Here 'def.aff.' refers to the Definitions of the Affects Spinoza presents at the end of Part Three of the *Ethics*.
25 Debray, 'Imitation des affects et production de l'ordre social', 163.

26 Spinoza, *Tractatus Theologico-Politicus*, 3:510.
27 Debray, 'Imitation des affects et production de l'ordre social', 164.
28 Wrangham, *The Goodness Paradox*, 220.
29 Spinoza, *Oeuvres*, vol. 3, 60.
30 Bootle, *This Is Not Who I Am*, 17.
31 Matheron calls it 'unsocial sociability' – Matheron, *Politics, Ontology and Knowledge in Spinoza*, 119–20.
32 Robinson, *The Cultural Revolution in China*, 30.
33 Debray, 'Imitation des affects et production de l'ordre social', 162–3.
34 Crisp, *Naked Civil Servant, Etc.*, 126.
35 Douglas, *Philosophy of Hope*, chap. 3.
36 Ibid.
37 Girardot, *Myth and Meaning in Early Daoism*, 77–8.
38 Hua, *China in Ten Words*, 186.
39 Sinclair, *I, Candidate for Governor*, 109.

6. *Beatitude*

1 Boethius, 'Consolation of Philosophy', 3.2.43–4.
2 Boethius, 3.3.3–6.
3 Pascal, *Pensées and Other Writings*, 10.148.
4 Ibid.
5 Jarrett, 'Spinozistic Constructivism', 63; James, *Spinoza on Learning to Live Together*, 184–5; Douglas, *Philosophy of Hope*, chap. 5.
6 Douglas, *Philosophy of Hope*, chap. 5; Douglas, 'Spinoza's Theophany: The Expression of God's Nature by Particular Things'.
7 Ziporyn, *Ironies of Oneness and Difference*, 166.
8 *Principles of Philosophy*, §51–4, AT 8A.24–5.
9 *Comments on a Certain Broadsheet*, AT 8B.349.

10 I provide this elsewhere: Douglas, *Philosophy of Hope*, chap. 5; Douglas, 'Spinoza's Theophany: The Expression of God's Nature by Particular Things'.
11 *Fifth Replies* AT 7.365.
12 Harold H. Joachim, *A Study of the Ethics of Spinoza: Ethica Ordine Geometrico Demonstrata* (Oxford: Clarendon Press, 1901), 104.
13 Douglas, 'Spinoza's Theophany: The Expression of God's Nature by Particular Things'.
14 Ibn al-'Arabī, *Al-Fūtūhat al-Makkiyah* (Cairo, 1911), 3.162.23. For further explanation see Chittick, *Self-Disclosure of God*, xxii. We do not have to worry about God failing to exist *as undetermined* if, as proposed, this is a logical impossibility.
15 Douglas, 'Spinoza's Theophany: The Expression of God's Nature by Particular Things'; Douglas, *Philosophy of Hope*, 66.
16 Ibn al-'Arabi, *Ringstones of Wisdom*, trans. Caner Dagli (Chicago: Kazi, 2004), 'Ringstone on the Wisdom of Unity in the Word of Hud', 97.
17 Infinite *what*? Spinoza does not say; the original is just '*infinita infinitis modis*' leaving interpreters puzzled (Spinoza, *Oeuvres*, vol. 3, 124). Most translate '*infinita*' as meaning 'infinitely many things'. In any case, on my reading Spinoza is stating that God's infinite nature requires him to exist in infinitely many determinate ways – that is *as* every possible thing.
18 Kamal, 'Ibn 'Arabi and Spinoza on God and the World'.
19 Al-Attas, 'The Mysticism of Hamzah Fansuri', 65.
20 *Fourth Replies*, AT 7.240.
21 Technically, Spinoza violates the principle of the Indiscernibility of Identicals, which holds that if A and B are *qualitatively* distinct, then they must be *numerically* distinct (not to be confused with the more controversial converse rule known as the Identity of Indiscernibles, which holds that numerically distinct things must

differ in their qualities). See Baxter, 'The Discernibility of Identicals'; Morrison, 'Two Puzzles about Thought and Identity in Spinoza'.

22 And, I believe, in Ibn 'Arabī. See the discussions of the 'perfect man' in Izutsu, *Sufism and Taoism*.

23 Wu, *The Butterfly as Companion*, 206.

24 Douglas, *Philosophy of Hope*, 103–8.

25 Douglas, 75–85.

26 Tan, 'Guo Xiang's Ontology of Zide', 12.

27 My predecessor at St Andrews, James Ferrier, wrote in a letter: 'The ego is an infinite and active capacity of *never being anything in particular*. [. . .] Depend on it, that is the true nature of a spirit – never to be any determinate existence. This is our real immutability – for death can get hold only of that which has determinate being' – Haldane, *James Frederick Ferrier*, 86.

28 *Passions of the Soul* 2.172: Descartes, *Philosophical Writings*, 1.391.

29 Han, *A Many-Splendoured Thing*, 40.

30 Ibid., 109.

31 The reference is to Henrik Ibsen's 1876 play, *Peer Gynt*, Act 5, Scene 5.

32 Han, *A Many-Splendoured Thing*, 124. In her autobiography, she asks: 'which one of those many mes would be the forever me? And once that fixed star of self-completion was reached, would my bones at last become resigned?' – Han, *My House Has Two Doors*, 25.

33 Han, *A Many-Splendoured Thing*, 334.

34 Ibid., 88.

35 Ibid., 207.

36 Chen, *In Praise of Nothing*, 90–92.

37 Ibid., 100.

38 Ibid., 102.

39 This is another Daoist reference, to the title of Chapter Two of the *Zhuangzi: Qiwulun* 齊物論 ('On Regarding All Things Equal') – discussed above.

40 Han, *A Many-Splendoured Thing*, 334.

41 The school of Tiantai Buddhism is another matter, at least according to Ziporyn, who makes it seem very close to the sort of thinking explored here: Ziporyn, *Emptiness and Omnipresence*.

42 Garfield, *Losing Ourselves*, 3.

43 Ibid., 12.

44 Ibid., 155.

45 Ibid., 39, 132.

46 Ibid., 8.

47 Ibid., 9.

48 I mean no insult by this; Garfield is a very successful author perhaps known to Hawking. Assume otherwise for the sake of argument.

7. Postmodern Paris to Silicon Valley

1 The first intellectual biography of Girard is: Haven, *Evolution of Desire*.

2 Girard, *Deceit, Desire, and the Novel*; Girard, *Battling to the End*.

3 Haven, *Evolution of Desire*, 195.

4 Gianfranco Mormino makes a compelling case that Girard's rejection of philosophy is based on a 'simplification', which 'ignores the existence of a current of thinking' running against the dominant Platonic tradition and represented especially by Spinoza: Mormino, 'Dal desiderio infantile alla religione: Spinoza e Girard'.

5 Girard, *Evolution and Conversion*, 18.

6 Sartre, *Existentialism is a Humanism*, 22.
7 Ibid., 29.
8 Bakewell, *Existentialist Café*, 154.
9 Ibid., 10.
10 Fanon, *The Wretched of the Earth*, 311.
11 Ibid., 312.
12 Ibid., 312.
13 Ibid., 315.
14 Lubis, *Twilight in Jakarta*, 34.
15 Ibid., 41.
16 Ibid., 139.
17 The work of the historian Jonathan Israel has been at the centre of controversy concerning Spinoza's relationship with the Enlightenment: Israel, *Radical Enlightenment*; Israel, *Enlightenment Contested*; Israel, *Democratic Enlightenment*; Israel, *The Enlightenment That Failed*; Israel, *Spinoza, Life and Legacy*.
18 Mishra, *Age of Anger*, 111.
19 Ibid., 90.
20 Ibid., 169–70.
21 Ibid., 176–7.
22 Hobsbawm and Ranger, *The Invention of Tradition*.
23 Mishra, *Age of Anger*, 175–6.
24 Haven, *Evolution of Desire*, 33.
25 Cayley, *The Ideas of René Girard*, 5.
26 Girard, *Violence and the Sacred*; Girard, *Things Hidden Since the Foundation of the World*; Girard, *The Scapegoat*; Girard, *I See Satan Fall Like Lightning*; Girard, *A Theatre of Envy*; Girard, *Anorexia and Mimetic Desire*; Girard, *Battling to the End*; Girard, *Sacrifice*.
27 Girard, *Deceit, Desire, and the Novel*, 15.
28 Sartre, *Existentialism is a Humanism*, 29.
29 Girard, *Violence and the Sacred*.
30 Ibid., 164.

31 Ibid., 165.
32 Ibid., 266.
33 Ibid., 347.
34 Ibid., 266–7.
35 Girard, *The Scapegoat*, 18.
36 Girard, *All Desire is a Desire for Being*, 144.
37 Haven, *Evolution of Desire*, chap. 7.
38 Girard, *I See Satan Fall Like Lightning*, 44; Weil, *First and Last Notebooks*, 147.
39 Girard, *Things Hidden Since the Foundation of the World*, 131.
40 Alison, *The Joy of Being Wrong*.
41 Girard, *Battling to the End*, xvii.
42 Girard, *All Desire is a Desire for Being*, 4.
43 Beauvoir, *The Ethics of Ambiguity*.
44 Ibid., 11.
45 The idea of indeterminacy somehow determining itself, without cause or reason, reminds me of Robert Neville's radical theological idea of pure creation from nothing; see Neville, *God the Creator*, 75.
46 The novelist and philosopher Iris Murdoch points out the subtle incoherence in holding that humans are both radically free and subject to an ethical responsibility – Murdoch, *Existentialists and Mystics*, 122–3. In her most famous book, *The Second Sex*, Beauvoir even speaks of the denial of freedom as a 'moral fault' and an 'absolute evil' – difficult words to reconcile with the background assertion that the world contains no absolute values beyond those the human subject creates by choosing – Beauvoir, *The Second Sex*, 37.
47 Beauvoir, *The Ethics of Ambiguity*, 71.
48 Girard, 'Memoirs of a Dutiful Existentialist'; Beauvoir, *Memoirs of a Dutiful Daughter*.
49 Girard, 'Memoirs of a Dutiful Existentialist', 53.

50 Girard, 54.
51 Bakewell, *Existentialist Café*, 13.
52 Girard, 'Memoirs of a Dutiful Existentialist', 55.
53 Girard, *When These Things Begin*, 110.
54 Girard, *The Scapegoat*; Girard, *A Theatre of Envy*.
55 Feloni, 'Peter Thiel Explains How an Esoteric Philosophy Book Shaped His Worldview'.
56 Naughton, 'Steve Jobs'. One person to whom Jobs was a mimetic model was Elizabeth Holmes, whose drive for success as a technology entrepreneur led her on a path that ended in an eleven-year prison sentence for fraud. During the days of her stardom, Holmes was often photographed wearing a black turtleneck – Jobs's trademark costume – also, as we have seen, the costume of the self-inventing existentialist. See Carreyrou, *Bad Blood*.
57 Girard, *When These Things Begin*, 71.
58 Marwick, *Status Update*, 166.
59 Mishra, *Run and Hide*.
60 Girard, *When These Things Begin*, 125.

8. Desiring Otherwise

1 Girard, 133.
2 Augustine, *Confessions*, 1997, 2.9, 67–8.
3 Ibid., 68n32.
4 Ibid., 2.12, 70.
5 Ibid., 2.14, 71.
6 Ibid., 2.16, 72.
7 Ibid., 2.17, 73.
8 Dupuy, *Le Sacrifice et l'envie – le libéralisme aux prises avec la justice sociale*, 268. In organizational psychology, this is known as the 'Abilene paradox': Harvey, 'The Abilene Paradox'.

9 Ko, *Non-Hierarchical Way*, 179.
10 Landy, 'Deceit, Desire, and the Literature Professor', 3.
11 Girard, *Violence and the Sacred*, 164.
12 Girard, *Deceit, Desire, and the Novel*, 53.
13 Ibid., 88.
14 Landy, 'Deceit, Desire, and the Literature Professor', 9.
15 Ibid., 3.
16 Girard, *Violence and the Sacred*, 164.
17 Landy, 'Deceit, Desire, and the Literature Professor', 3.
18 Girard, *Deceit, Desire, and the Novel*, 6.
19 Wiggins, 'Deliberation and Practical Reason', 50n5.
20 Sartre refers to this idea as the 'spirit of seriousness': Sartre, *Being and Nothingness*, 809–10.
21 Moeller and D'Ambrosio, *You and Your Profile*, 26.
22 See Chapter 3, footnote 38.
23 Carroll, *The Annotated Alice*, 224.
24 Girard, *All Desire is a Desire for Being*, 204.
25 Girard, *Deceit, Desire, and the Novel*, 66.
26 Ibid., 56.
27 Ibid.
28 Sartre, *Being and Nothingness*, 735.
29 Ibid.
30 Ibid., 797.
31 Girard, *Deceit, Desire, and the Novel*, 57.
32 Ibid., 73.
33 On Girard's theory as applied to early childhood, see Oughourlian, *The Puppet of Desire*; Alison, *The Joy of Being Wrong*, 27–33.
34 Girard, *I See Satan Fall Like Lightning*, 15.
35 Girard, *Deceit, Desire, and the Novel*; Girard, *Resurrection from the Underground*.
36 Girard, *Deceit, Desire, and the Novel*, 256.
37 Dostoevsky, *Notes from Underground*, 28.

38 Ibid., 24.
39 Ibid., 35.
40 Girard, *Deceit, Desire, and the Novel*, 257.
41 Dostoevsky, *Notes from Underground*, 56.
42 Ibid., 59.
43 Girard, *Deceit, Desire, and the Novel*, 54.
44 Girard, *Resurrection from the Underground*, 18.
45 Luke 23:11–12, Girard, *Things Hidden Since the Foundation of the World*, 187.
46 Again, there is much more to his account than I have the space to relate here. For Girard, the Christian revelation, whose full effect is still only beginning to be felt, establishes a radical rupture between the ancient and the modern world. Some useful sources on this are: Bailie, *Violence Unveiled*; Kirwan, *Discovering Girard*; Palaver, *René Girard's Mimetic Theory*; Cowdell, *René Girard and Secular Modernity*; Cayley, *The Ideas of René Girard*.
47 Girard, *Evolution and Conversion*, 58.
48 Ibid.
49 Girard, *Things Hidden Since the Foundation of the World*, 283–4.
50 Ibid., 292.
51 Baumeister, *Evil*, 244.
52 Girard, *Things Hidden Since the Foundation of the World*, 274.

9. *Salvation and the Imitation of Jesus*

1 Girard, *Evolution and Conversion*, 43.
2 Girard, *I See Satan Fall Like Lightning*, 15.
3 Ibid.
4 Masters and Thiel, *Zero to One*, 28.
5 Girard, *Mimesis and Theory*, 239.

6 Pogue, 'Inside the New Right, Where Peter Thiel is Placing His Biggest Bets'.
7 Girard, *Battling to the End*, 18.
8 Girard, *Things Hidden Since the Foundation of the World*, 274.
9 Deleuze and Guattari, *Anti-Oedipus*, 162.
10 Girard, *To Double Business Bound*, 84.
11 Srinivasan, *The Right to Sex*, 91.
12 Girard, *Violence and the Sacred*, chap. 7.
13 Ibid., 192–3.
14 Ibid., 195.
15 Ibid., 203.
16 Ibid.
17 Girard, *To Double Business Bound*, 91.
18 Girard, *Deceit, Desire, and the Novel*, 9.
19 Girard, *Things Hidden Since the Foundation of the World*, 274.
20 Girard, *Deceit, Desire, and the Novel*, 111.
21 Ibid., 222–3.
22 Ibid., 293–4.
23 Ibid., 294.
24 Ibid.
25 Ibid., 295.
26 Girard, *Resurrection from the Underground*, 66.
27 Girard, *Battling to the End*, 101.
28 The thesis that modern culture is much more fundamentally Christian than it recognizes has also been pursued by the social critic Ivan Illich and the historian Tom Holland: Illich and Cayley, *The Rivers North of the Future*; Holland, *Dominion*.
29 Girard, *I See Satan Fall Like Lightning*, 13.
30 Girard, *Battling to the End*, 120.
31 Girard, *I See Satan Fall Like Lightning*, 14.
32 Ko, *Non-Hierarchical Way*, chap. 8.

33 Ko, 182.
34 Girard, *I See Satan Fall Like Lightning*, 14.
35 Girard, *Resurrection from the Underground*, 66.
36 Girard, *Battling to the End*, 123. The translator has 'Him', with a capital H, but this implies that the pronoun stands for Christ rather than the other, which is belied by the next sentence in the text.
37 Ibid., 133.
38 Ibid., 34–5, 45–8, 94, 212.
39 Ibid., 46–7.
40 Ko, *Non-Hierarchical Way*, 186.
41 Ibid., 184.
42 Girard, *Sacrifice*, chap. 2; Klostermaier, *A Survey of Hinduism*, 87. See note 4 in the Introduction.
43 Sinclair, *A Defence of Idealism*, 335.
44 Girard, *Battling to the End*, 201.

Conclusion: Against Identity

1 Haldane, *James Frederick Ferrier*, 86.
2 Tagore, *The Religion of Man*, 188.
3 Unamuno, *Tragic Sense of Life*, 90.
4 Douglas, *Philosophy of Hope*, 128.
5 Kasser, *The High Price of Materialism*, chap. 5; Storr, *Selfie*; Moeller and D'Ambrosio, *You and Your Profile*; Han, *The Transparency Society*.
6 Paley, *Beyond Bad*, chap. 8.
7 McCloskey, *Why Liberalism Works*; Phelps, *Mass Flourishing*; Cockshott, *How the World Works*, sec. 7.1; Phelps et al., *A Vital People*; Ridley, *How Innovation Works*, chap. 12; Erixon and Weigel, *The Innovation Illusion*; Hall, *Where Is My Flying Car?*

8 Hannah Ritchie points out that reaching sustainability, as defined by the United Nations, would be an *unprecedented* human achievement: previously human populations have either failed to sufficiently supply their needs (i.e. endured devastating levels of infant and adult mortality) or done so in an ecologically unsustainable way – Ritchie, *Not the End of the World*, chap. 1.

9 Naughton, 'Steve Jobs'.

10 Borges, *The Borges Reader*, 285.

11 Yunkaporta, *Sand Talk*, 99.

12 Mishra, *Age of Anger*, 346.

Index